My

My Favourite Lévi-Strauss

edited by
Dipankar Gupta

YODA PRESS

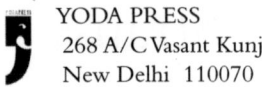
YODA PRESS
268 A/C Vasant Kunj
New Delhi 110070

Published in India
by YODA PRESS

© Dipankar Gupta 2011

The moral rights of the author have been asserted
Database right YODA PRESS (maker)

First Published 2011

All rights reserved. No part of this publication may be reproduced, stored in a retrieval system, or transmitted, in any form or by any means, without the prior permission in writing of YODA PRESS, or as expressly permitted by law, or under the terms agreed with the appropriate reprographics rights organisation. Enquiries concerning reproduction outside the scope of the above should be sent to YODA PRESS, at the address above.

You must not circulate this book in any other binding or cover and you must impose the same condition on any acquirer.

ISBN 978-93-80403-13-7

Typeset in Bembo Std 11/14.4
By Jojy Philip, New Delhi 110 015
Printed at Japan Art Press, New Delhi 110 028
Published by Arpita Das for YODA PRESS, New Delhi

Contents

The Making of 'My Favourite Lévi-Strauss' *Dipankar Gupta*	vii
Claude Lévi-Strauss: A Rationalist among Empiricists *André Béteille*	1
Claude Lévi-Strauss: His Life and Work *Philippe Descola*	5
To Transform or to Transmorph: From Totemism to Traffic Lights to Caste *Dipankar Gupta*	16
Why a Cousin Becomes a Spouse: Elementary, says Lévi-Strauss *Rita Brara*	43
Claude Lévi-Strauss, 2008: What Anniversary? *Vincent Debaene*	61
Mythologique: The Structural Method of Claude Lévi-Strauss *Harjeet Singh Gill*	76
Lévi-Strauss or Sartre? Kant and the Savage Mind *Pradeep A. Dhillon*	89

On Language and the Assumed Unity of
the Human Sciences   101
    Franson Manjali

'Naming' Conversion: Being Muslim in Old Delhi   118
    Deepak Mehta

Lévi-Strauss and Evolutionary Theory   145
    Maurice Bloch

Appendix   159

The Making of 'My Favourite Lévi-Strauss'

In celebrating the 100th birthday of Professor Claude Lévi-Strauss, we are giving ourselves the opportunity to revive a major inspirational fount of much of our received knowledge as anthropologists. For more than five decades, Professor Lévi-Strauss has influenced professional anthropologists, and indeed scholars in all the social sciences through his wide ranging researches, made all the more remarkable by his novel explication of structuralism. One can easily say that after Lévi-Strauss, the way we think can never be the same.

Quite like the myths he wrote about with such finesse, Lévi-Strauss's own works have devotees and followers who lean more heavily on this or that text of the master. We all have our *favourite* Lévi-Strauss who stands by our side guiding our research and teaching with the complete conviction that there is a unity that binds humankind.

Accordingly, in the conference on which this volume is based, the contributors did not attempt to write essays on the lines of 'what-Lévi-Strauss-really-meant', but rather in the spirit of being inspired by him in ways that would otherwise have escaped their imagination. There is, therefore, no attempt at orthodoxy, or even a puritanical rendition of structuralism. Our authors have written on a wide variety of themes, but in every case, Lévi-Strauss's imprint is very visible in ways that they perhaps never suspected themselves.

In keeping with the spirit of the conference, the essays presented here have no intention of interpreting Lévi-Strauss 'correctly', or in debating over what he 'really said', but rather on what he meant to us in our active commitment as professional anthropologists. I believe this is in keeping with the profound effect Lévi-Strauss has had on all of us. Consequently, it is difficult to say where the master left off and the disciples carried on.

As an organizer of this conference on Lévi-Strauss's 100th birthday what gave me the greatest satisfaction was the near 100 per cent acceptance rate of our invited speakers. Apart from being intimate with Lévi-Strauss's work, they are some of the best scholars in the world. It is not as if they received a lot of notice, but they were happy to participate primarily because they felt for the cause they were celebrating.

We were lucky in getting all the help we needed from the Centre de Sciences Humaines of the French Embassy in New Delhi. The idea of celebrating Lévi-Strauss's 100th birthday came up in a conversation with the Ambassador of France, H.E. Jerome Bonnafont one summer evening. He expressed a strong desire to do something in India to celebrate Lévi Strauss's remarkable achievements at a time when he had just turned 100. I could not have agreed with him more. Lévi-Strauss has been one of the most important intellectual influences in my life and he has never failed me in all these years.

I first read *The Savage Mind* when I was quite young, just about to step out of my teens. I have always felt, that Lévi-Strauss, like Marx, should be introduced to scholars when their minds are nimble and imaginative. I am probably generalizing from my own experience, but it is a lesson I find hard to ignore. In my long career as a teacher, I did what I could to bring Lévi-Strauss to the attention of my students at the earliest opportunity. One is never too young to start cultivating the imagination that Lévi-Strauss invites us to participate in.

At any rate, the idea of holding a conference in Delhi took root because H.E. Jerome Bonnafont not only expressed a desire to sponsor such an event, but also made available the resources of his Embassy, and in particular, the CSH for this purpose.

Once we were certain that the conference would be held I had the good fortune of Professor André Béteille's advice. That he agreed to open the celebrations with Ambassador, Jerorme Bonnafont, certainly added to the lustre of the occasion. All our star speakers had submitted their presentations and were ready to go. I knew from the start that this would be a very memorable gathering, but my confidence in my prediction kept growing as the minutes ticked by.

Marielle Morin and Dhritabrata Bhattacharjya (Tato) worked very hard to get the conference off the ground. We aimed for some of the best minds and got them to come to Delhi. This, in itself, was triumph enough. What exceeded our expectations was the tremendous turnout in every session. Citizens of Delhi just poured in to the India International Centre, where the conference was being held. Their ready and keen participation in the discussions added to the enthusiasm of the gathering. It was truly a birthday party of very impressive proportions, and this volume is an apt reminder of that occasion.

Along with Ms. Morin and Mr. Bhattacharya, a large number of students from the Jawaharlal Nehru University gave their time to make sure that the logistics were right, the arrangements just so and the audience in good humour. They worked long hours, travelled long distances in Delhi's hazardous traffic, to take news of the conference to different parts of the city and to make sure that students and teachers from other institutions did not face too much trouble in getting to the India International Centre. There are just too many students who put in time, money and effort during those days to mention individually, but I need to acknowledge here just a few. Sreedeep Bhattacharya led the charge, but he was ably helped along the way by Arnab Roy Choudhuri, Yogesh Kumar, Ankita Mukherjee, Ritu Sharma, Tapasi Malhotra, and Sumedha Dutta, among several others.

At the India International Centre one could not have asked for greater co-operation. Premola Ghose's support was invaluable. She was not only wholly on our side, but made sure that the Lévi-Strauss conference went without a hitch. This required a lot of effort on her part, but she held course all the way. We often moved venues within the India International Centre, changed the number of guests who were going to stay there and also the lunch and tea arrangements, but she helped us through all these difficulties with perfect élan, enthusiasm and efficiency.

Finally, I must thank Yoda Press for doing such a splendid job. Arpita Das took charge of this project and delivered it on time and without sacrificing quality at any point.

This volume should, hopefully, become a standard reference book in Sociology and Social Anthropology, particularly for post graduate and research scholars. Veteran teachers of many years too should find the essays here useful and inspiring. I, for myself, learnt a lot from these essays and I hope the readers will also feel that they have been equally fortunate.

DIPANKAR GUPTA

Claude Lévi-Strauss
A Rationalist among Empiricists*

André Béteille

The passing of Claude Lévi-Strauss (1908–2009) marks the end of an era in the study of human culture. He was in his time the most renowned anthropologist in the world, and perhaps more renowned than any other anthropologist at any time or in any place. But he was much more than that. He was a pioneer of a whole intellectual movement that came to be known as 'structuralism', and his thought influenced scholars and writers in many different fields. My sense is that his standing as a man of letters in France will outlive his technical innovations as an anthropologist.

Lévi-Strauss's first major contribution to anthropology was a work on kinship published originally in 1949. That work, entitled *The Elementary Structures of Kinship*, took time to secure worldwide attention since an English translation did not appear until twenty years later. To the English-speaking anthropologists who read it in the original, the arguments of the book appeared strange and unfamiliar, and its theoretical claims too sweeping. But it did secure a commanding position in course of time, and came to be much admired even by those who had little knowledge of the literature on kinship.

* This essay first appeared in *The Telegraph*.

The Elementary Structures propounded a new approach to the study of kinship that came to be known as 'alliance theory' as against the 'descent theory' favoured by the British anthropologists who had dominated the field until then. Descent theory focuses on the transmission of rights and obligations across the generations, whereas alliance theory dwells on the chains of relations established by matrimonial exchange between bride-givers and bride-takers. An early proponent of alliance theory in the study of Indian kinship was Louis Dumont, the author of a magisterial work on caste.

Like other anthropologists before him, Lévi-Strauss assigned great significance to the incest rule, but gave a new twist to the interpretation of that rule. He argued that it should not be viewed only negatively, but also positively; not just as a prohibition, but, above all, as a prescription. A man is not told simply that he must not marry his own sister, he is asked to give his sister in marriage to another man and, in turn, to receive someone else's sister as his wife. In Lévi-Strauss's own words, 'the prohibition of incest is a rule of reciprocity'. Exchange and reciprocity, which constitute the core of social life, follow directly from the incest rule, hence its great social significance. Lévi-Strauss would go so far as to say that it was that rule that provided the first foundation of social life among human beings.

Lévi-Strauss's great gift was the gift of imagination, and he was a master of the art of interpreting symbols. As such, his best work was not his work on kinship, but his work on mythology. It was through a series of studies of the myths of primitive people that he gave free rein to his talent for demonstrating unsuspected, not to say startling, connections among symbols, and established his position as a structuralist. He was a rationalist who took a lofty, not to say disdainful, view of the empiricist bias in most of Anglo-American anthropology. If such a distinction is permissible, he always chose ideas over facts, and symbolic, as against utilitarian, interpretations.

Shortly before he launched on his massive enterprise on the study of myths, he published a brief study of totemism, which had been a favourite subject among anthropologists since the end of the 19th century. Earlier anthropologists, particularly in Britain, had been inclined to argue that among primitive people totemism fulfilled the function of ensuring the maintenance and reproduction of plant and animal species. Lévi-Strauss insisted that its primary significance was to provide symbolic markers for the differentiation of human groups through the differentiation of the natural world.

Lévi-Strauss saw himself not just as a rationalist but also as an explorer in far-away places among little-known people. Not long after his work on kinship, he published a book called *Tristes tropiques* in French and *A World on the Wane* in English. It is a fascinating and tantalizing book, part travelogue, part ethnography and part philosophical speculation. Because that book was translated into English before the book on kinship, and because of its richly evocative literary style, it received more attention than *The Elementary Structures of Kinship*. Lévi-Strauss's many admirers in India should know that he has not always been well served by his English translators.

If his studies of kinship and myth bring out the rationalist in Lévi-Strauss, *Tristes tropiques* brings out the romantic in him. In it, he gives us glimpses into the lives of some of the forest-dwelling communities of the Amazon basin: the Bororo, the Caduveo, the Nambikwara and others. Their technological equipment might not be much to boast of, but their tattoos, their folk tales and their mythology show a richness and variety that is almost inexhaustible. Lévi-Strauss has done more than any other anthropologist to show that the poverty of material technology need not be an impediment to the proliferation of an exuberant symbolic life.

The standard method of fieldwork established by Malinowski and his followers came to be known as the method of 'participant-observation'. It is respected, though not always faithfully followed, by anthropologists in most countries, including India. Lévi-Strauss has insisted on the maintenance of distance between the observer and the observed as an essential part of the work of the anthropologist. There is little place in this scheme of things for the anthropologist to go native. Perhaps this was his way of showing respect for the communities about which he wrote. On the other hand, the British anthropologists of his generation whom I knew, such as Meyer Fortes and Max Gluckman, had little praise for the quality and reliability of his empirical material.

The relationship between anthropology and sociology has been a subject of debate and discussion among students of society and culture throughout the world, and particularly in India. Few scholars have expressed themselves more clearly and consistently on the subject than Lévi-Strauss. For him, sociology is the study of one's own society, in his case French (or European) society, whereas anthropology is the study of other cultures. As he sees it, what is distinctive of anthropology as a discipline is not any peculiarity of the communities it studies but the relationship of the investigator to the object of his investigation. In his own striking words, "The anthropologist is the astronomer of the social sciences."

The natural tendency among students of society and culture in India has been to stress not the separation between sociology and anthropology, but their unity. This is as true of G.S. Ghurye as of M.N. Srinivas or S.C. Dube. N.K. Bose began his career by studying a small tribe of shifting cultivators in Orissa, and later made a masterful study of the social structure of his own city, Calcutta. For him, the unity of sociology and social anthropology followed directly from the belief in the unity of India. This presents a paradox to the Indian followers of Lévi-Strauss who have sometimes adopted the subterfuge of being sociologists at home and anthropologists abroad, where the study of Indian society, no matter by whom, is a part of anthropology, not sociology.

Claude Lévi-Strauss
His Life and Work

Philippe Descola

Claude Lévi-Strauss, born in Brussels on 28 November 1908 to French parents, is undoubtedly the anthropologist whose work has had the greatest influence on the twentieth century. After his secondary and higher studies in Paris, (masters in law, aggregation in philosophy in 1931), he was appointed philosophy teacher at the Mont-de-Marsan and then Laon (1932–34) high schools. He was a member of the French University mission to Brazil (along with Fernand Braudel and Pierre Deffontaines, in particular), he taught sociology and ethnology from 1935 to 1938 at the newly created Sao Paulo University and carried out several ethnographic expeditions in the Mato Grosso, then in the Amazon, before returning to France on the eve of the war, during which he acted as a liaison agent. When he was demobilized after the armistice, Lévi-Strauss became a victim of the Vichy anti-Semitic laws; however, he managed to leave France for the United States where he taught at the New School for Social Research in New York. He voluntarily joined the Forces françaises libres/ Free French forces, and was assigned to the scientific mission in the United States, he founded, (along with Henri Focillon, Alexandre Koyré and Jacques Maritain, amongst others), the Ecole libre des hautes études in New York and became its general secretary. The Ministry of Foreign Affairs brought him back to France in 1944; he returned however, to the United States in 1945 as cultural advisor with the French Embassy. On his return to France in 1948, Lévi-Strauss defended his doctoral thesis on *Les structures élémentaires de la parenté* (his secondary thesis was on *La vie familiale et sociale des Indiens Nambikwara*) and from then on he dedicated himself entirely to his scientific work. In 1948 Lucien Febvre invited him to join the newly created 6th section of the École pratique des hautes études (that became the École des hautes études en sciences sociales in 1975). Lévi-Strauss became assistant director of the musée de l'Homme in 1949 and the same year, was appointed study supervisor at the 5th section of the École pratique des hautes études, to the chair of comparative religions of peoples without writing. He went on to become a professor at the Collège de France, occupying the social anthropology chair from 1959 till he retired in 1982. Throughout his time there, he directed the social anthropology Laboratory that he had founded in 1960. In 1973, he became a member of the Académie française.

Claude Lévi-Strauss's name is synonymous with what came to be later known as structural anthropology. In the variety of approaches the field of social sciences knew during the twentieth century, the structural approach occupied a singular position: it was neither an audacious rereading of an already recognized explanatory system, nor a regional theory of a category of circumscribed phenomena; it was primarily an original method of knowledge, developed out of the handling of problems specific to a discipline, but where the object was so vast and the fecundity so remarkable, that it rapidly exercised its influence far beyond the field of research in which it was born. An analytical model of social facts has rarely been so closely linked to the person who created it, to the extent that anthropological structuralism sometimes seemed to be a thought system that could not be employed by anyone other than its creator. Lévi-Strauss formulated its principles while he was in the

United States, after he had discovered structural linguistics and N. Trouvetzkoy and R. Jakobson's work (the latter, whom he met in New York, became a friend). In fact, at this time, he was already convinced that ethnology had to follow the same path as linguistics if it wanted to acquire the status of a rigorous science.[1]

His familiarity with his 'three mistresses'—Freud, Marx and geology—also convinced him, very early on, that social science could not be built upon manifest reality, but by elucidating the unconscious order, where the rational coincidence between the properties of thought and those of the world were revealed, in phonology, he discovered an exemplary model by which to implement his intuition. This model possesses four remarkable characteristics: it abandons the level of conscious phenomena in favour of a study of their unconscious infrastructure; it does not take terms as its object of analysis, but rather the relationships that connect them; it tries to show that these relationships form a system; last, it aims to discover general laws. As early as this, Lévi-Strauss made the hypothesis that, combined, these four approaches could help shed light on the problems of kinship due to the formal analogy he saw between phonemes and terms that were used to designate relations. Both are elements whose significance is drawn from the fact of being combined in systems, themselves products of the unconscious functioning of the mind, and their recurrence in innumerable places in the world suggests that they follow universal laws.

All the key ideas of structural anthropology are already present in this outline, including the concept of exchange that comes from a different intellectual inheritance, Marcel Mauss's 'Essai sur le don'

---

[1] 'L'analyse structurale en linguistique et en anthropologie', *Word, Journal of the Linguistic Circle of New-York*, vol. 1, no. 2, August 1945, pp. 1–21; republished in *Anthropologie structurale*, Paris, Plon, 1958, chap. II.

that occupied front stage in *Les structures élémentaires de la parenté*. At the beginning of this book, Lévi-Strauss postulates that the prohibition of incest must be seen as the universal and negative reverse of a rule of positive reciprocity that orders the exchange of women in matrimonial alliance systems. This perspective radically renewed the approach to kinship phenomena, abandoning the sociological viewpoint of modes of lineage and principles behind the constitution of descent groups, like that of their conjectural historical reconstruction, that functionalism and evolutionism had limited themselves to until this time. It substituted a general theory of marriage alliance that, in return, shed light on the nature and functioning of the social groups involved in kinship—clans, lineages, exogamous groups—while resituating them as part of a wider whole. It also established the generality and recurrence of rules that organize the systems of matrimonial exchanges along mental structures—the only logical basis that, according to Lévi-Strauss, made it possible to safeguard the premise of the unity of man in the diversity of his cultural productions. This can be seen from the dualist organization, a very common system in which the members of the community are divided into two halves that maintain a whole range of complex relationships of interdependence. The institution clearly reveals the classificatory mechanisms of kinship—each one defines itself by it's belonging to a half—and beyond, the crucial role of the principle of reciprocity, where the dualist organization seems to be the most direct realization, but it can also be incarnated in numerous other forms of social life. Lévi-Strauss affirmed that between all these forms, there was a difference of degree and not of nature, as their common basis lay in fundamental structures of the human mind: the principle of reciprocity, the requirement of the rule as a rule and the synthetic nature of gift, that is to say the fact that the agreed transfer of the value of an individual to another transforms them into partners and adds a new quality to the transferred value.[2] Thus, it is clearly in man's nature, in formal and universal schema that are deeply inscribed in his mind, but not always consciously apprehended, that the basis of matrimonial institutions and at a wider level, culture itself, is located, the emergence of which can be seen from the prohibition of incest. Such a profession of faith is only idealistic in appearance, as early as *Les Structures élémentaires de la parenté*, and throughout his work, Lévi-Strauss affirmed his conviction that the laws of thought were no different from the laws that apply in the physical world and in social reality, that was itself only one aspect of it.

The title 'social anthropology' Lévi-Strauss had given to his course at the 6th section of the EPHE on his return to France is the same as the one he later used at the Collège de France. The choice of these terms defines aptly the change of perspective he brought to ethnological studies. While it had been in use for decades in Anglo-Saxon countries, the expression 'social anthropology' was uncommon in France at the end of the war; it evoked the universalistic project proper to philosophical anthropologies while also implying a hierarchy of modes and objects of knowledge, of which ethnography and ethnology were the other terms, not in a descending order of nobility, but depending on their internal structures in the different phases of the scientific approach.[3] Ethnography that is analytical and descriptive, corresponds to the early stages of research: it is fieldwork and collection of all kinds of data about a specific society that generally results in a monographic work, limited in time and space. Ethnology is a continuation of ethnography and represents a first effort towards synthesis, aiming towards generalizations that are sufficiently broad at a regional level (groups of neighbouring

---

[2] *Les Structures élémentaires de la parenté*, Paris, P.U.F., 1949, p. 108.

[3] See in particular *Anthropologie structurale, Paris, Librairie Plon,* 1958, pp. 386–89.

societies where affinities are visible) or thematic (attention paid to a type of phenomenon or practice common to numerous societies) so that the use of secondary ethnographic sources is a compulsory precondition and the updating of comparable qualities the expected result. Less often taken to fruition, anthropology represents the final part of the synthesis: on the basis of ethnographic and ethnological teaching, it aspires to produce a global knowledge of man by revealing principles that make the diversity of his social productions and cultural representations throughout the centuries and across the continents, intelligible.

Despite the title of his course at the 6th section, from the second half of the 1950s onwards, Lévi-Strauss worked towards privileging cultural anthropology rather than social anthropology. He remained faithful to his project of drawing up an inventory of 'mental compartments' based on ethnographic experience and convinced that anthropology was first a psychology, he progressively abandoned the field of sociological studies to dedicate himself to the study of different manifestations of mythical thought. In fact, nothing guarantees that the limitations revealed in kinship systems are of mental origin; maybe they are only the reflection in man's consciousness of 'certain requirements of social life, objectified in institutions'.[4] Mythology does not present this ambiguity, as it has no practical function and the analyst can thus discover, in a particularly pure form, the workings of a mind that is no longer condemned to organizing a reality that is external to it, but free to compose with itself as if through a division. The work on 'savage thought' constitutes an intermediary stage in this attempt to constantly move further towards the unconscious laws of the mind. The classification systems and ritual operations of societies without writing deal, of course, with objects, generally natural ones and

---

[4] *Mythologiques*, vol. 1, *Le cru et le cuit*, Paris, Plon, 1964, p. 18.

their presumed connections, but they also render manifest mental operations (classification, hierarchization, causality, homology) that do not fundamentally differ from those of scientific thought, even if the phenomena they deal with and the knowledge they produce can make them seem very distant. Savage thought is in fact first applied to sensitive categories, flushing out and organizing the most remarkable visible characteristics of natural objects, to convert them into signs of their hidden qualities. Unlike abstract concepts that science employs, these signs are still stuck to the images out of which they are born, but they nonetheless already possess a sufficient degree of autonomy with regard to their referents to be able to be used, within their limited register, for ends other than those for which they were initially intended. The logic of sensitive qualities is thus 'an intellectual bricolage' that exploits a limited directory of relationships that can be permutated within a group that forms a system, the 'transformation group', and in such a way that the modification of one of its elements will necessarily interest all the others. Thus, the ambition of structural analysis is not only to elucidate the hidden logic at work in mythical thought, what it aims at through the study of 'savage thought' is to understand the element of 'thought in a savage state' that each one of us contains within ourselves like a residue of the time before the general rational domestication.

In 1959, Claude Lévi-Strauss was elected professor to the Collège de France thanks to Maurice Merleau-Ponty's active intervention. This consecration sanctioned a work that was henceforth recognized and admired by a wide circle of scholars and intellectuals all over the world, but it also showed, *a contrario*, traditional universities' resistance to including within their system research that seemed too far removed from the orthodox approach. The use of the same title 'social anthropology' did not in any manner signify a return to sociological problems. The period that began now was in fact one of a study of myths and led to the publication of the four volumes of *Mythologiques*, over a period of eight years, for which the classes taught at the Collège de France provided the basis. Even more than other products of savage thought, myths seem to be the fruit of a creative freedom from the constraints of reality; the revelation of the laws that govern their functioning should thus allow us to go further towards the understanding of a mind that takes itself as the object without the subjects who are speaking being conscious of how they are doing it. Each myth taken separately is, in fact, an unreasonable story that has no true signification apart from the moral lesson that those who are telling it sometimes feel justified in revealing. This is because the meaning does not come from the content of one or the other myth that has been wrongly privileged, but from the thousands of myths echoing each other, that, beyond the apparent diversity of their content and the distance between the populations who created them, weave a logical framework in constant transformation, around the world, where the multiple combinations show the closed field of operations of the human mind. The structural analysis of myths can thus never claim to be exhaustive; it progresses following associations along a syntagmatic chain, from a reference myth that has been chosen arbitrarily, it can only aspire to carving out matrices of fragmented significations, within this vast framework, that another approach may have ignored. *Mythologies* is an account of an itinerary over the round world of myths; rather than the universal geography of their networks, it invites the reader to continue the journey that Lévi-Strauss himself was ceaselessly on.

Lévi-Strauss' vast scientific work should not let us forget the importance of his moral reflection: he tirelessly denounced the joint impoverishment of the diversity of cultures and natural species, he always saw anthropology as a critical instrument towards prejudice, particularly racial prejudice, while being a means of implementing a 'generalized' humanism, that is to say, no longer that of the Renaissance type, limited only to Western societies, but taking into account the experience and knowledge that all human societies, both past and present, possess. Far from leading towards an improbable global civilization that would abolish difference, on the contrary, this humanism takes into account that which at a material and spiritual level, any true creation imposes on an individual as on a culture, that is to draw upon their specificities in order to contrast them with other values. The aesthetic question is also a line that runs through Lévi-Strauss' thought, not only because he considered forms of artistic expression, or those that were perceived as such, from non-Western societies both a challenge to the West's rationality and a legitimate object of anthropological knowledge, but also because his work was enriched by a deep reflection on the role of music and painting as a mediation between the sensible and the intelligible that makes it a superb contribution to aesthetic theory.

The influence of structural anthropology developed in different ways depending on the times and types of intellectual circles it came into contact with. Just after the war, French ethnologists of Lévi-Strauss' generation (Soustelle, Giraule, Leroi-Gourhan) were themselves too involved in their own work to be deeply influenced by his ideas, so it was more abroad, in England and the Netherlands, in particular, that his ideas were first echoed. In France it was mainly linguists (Benveniste, Dumézil), philosophers (Koyré, Merleau-Ponty), historians (Febvre, Braudel, Morazé) who, at the beginning of the 1950s could appreciate the originality of the horizons Lévi-Strauss opened up. When *Tristes Tropiques* appeared in 1955, a more general public discovered the originality of Lévi-Strauss' work and the prose of a great writer; over a long period it contributed to encouraging a vocation for ethnology. Despite this, structural anthropology *stricto sensu* has no legitimate interpreter other than its founder, as no one abides by all the postulates, the rules of method and the conclusions that define the specificity of the Lévi-Straussian enterprise. There are, however, a large number of French researchers who can identify with what one could call structuralist ethnology, the homogeneity of which is better perceived from abroad because of the specificities it expresses in comparison to other national anthropological traditions. It can be distinguished by several characteristics, although their totality does not necessarily constitute a shared credo: the conviction that the task of anthropology is to elucidate the apparent variability of social and cultural phenomena by revealing minimal invariables, that is to say, recurring regularities in the organization of kinship systems between classes of objects or relationships whose functioning most often obeys unconscious rules; the hypothesis that theses invariables are based on material determinations (the structure of the brain, man's biological characteristics, the modalities of his productive activity or the physical qualities of the objects that make up his environment) and on certain trans-historical imperatives of social life; and last, the precedence accorded to synchronic analysis over diachronic analysis, not through a rejection of the historical dimension, but by the refusal of the empiricist position that consists of explaining the genesis of a system before having defined its structure.

Finally, and because it is a method of knowledge that can, in principle, be extended to cover any social and cultural phenomena, structural anthropology was also able to find an audience outside the field traditionally covered by ethnology; among certain philosophers, who were happy to accept a thought that rejected the primacy of consciousness and the subject (Merleau-Ponty, Foucault, Althusser, Deleuze); amongst historians too, those working on antiquity, medievalists and specialists of non-European societies in particular, were as seduced by Lévi-Strauss' method as by the temptation to apprehend their respective objects with the 'view from afar' that ethnologists adopt while carrying out research among an exotic people. It is true that historians like J.P. Vernant had been carrying out perfectly structural analyses for years and his influence combined with that of Dumézil and Lévi-Strauss decisively contributed to a certain 'structuralist orientation' of studies of Antiquity.

To Transform or to Transmorph
From Totemism to Traffic Lights to Caste

DIPANKAR GUPTA

How can one be deeply influenced by Claude Lévi-Strauss and yet not be a thorough structuralist? It has often been acknowledged that Lévi-Strauss inspires us in ways that he probably did not intend to. After we read him we suddenly become aware of our unexamined prejudices and some of our old verities appear more like cant than as certainties. This essay is a Lévi-Straussian-inspired treatment of caste which may perhaps not pass the strict canons of structuralism, but it should not be dismissed just for that. I believe a tribute to a guru is that much greater when it comes from those who are outside the close band of staunch followers.

What are those aspects of Lévi-Strauss that I find inspiring as I study caste in India? Lévi-Strauss not only wrote about caste, but he also wrote innovatively about it. His comparison between caste and totemism brought out details that even the best Indianists had not suspected. The fact that endogamy logically entails hierarchy is a reversal of what is generally believed to be the case. But there is much more we can mine from Lévi Strauss's scholarship as we make our way through the many arcane and tortuous passages of caste. Rarely need one explicitly return to his nuggets on this subject, but it is his method, and more, his inspiration that counts. Probably, Lévi-Strauss might even disapprove of this exercise, but I believe, in a Nietzschean vein, that misinterpretation is allowed if the end is good.

Imagination without Structuralism: Can one still be a Lévi-Straussian?

The most useful catechism of the structuralist method is to be found in Totemism (1962: 16). Here Lévi-Strauss advises that we take a phenomenon under study as a relation between two or more elements, real or *imagined*; then do a permutation of these relationships and finally consider the whole chart (including the imagined ones) as the object of analysis. Only Lévi-Strauss could confidently say that we should imagine a few relations to complete the picture for only he seems to know exactly which ones they should be.

Though such exercises may appear very personalized, the demonstration effect is impressive for the chart with real and imagined relations laid out for objective scrutiny. One may not have thought that the unit of kinship, for example, should include four relations. We now know, post Lévi-Strauss, that Radcliffe-Brown limited our understanding of the mother's brother by discussing only two relations, but should we stop at four? Why did Lévi-Strauss not press ahead and denote the basic unit of kinship in terms of six, or even eight, relations?

But if one were to put such doubts in abeyance and go along with Lévi-Strauss's own exposition then at the end of the day we learn something new. Even if some of these relations start their career as imaginary ones, they become credible once they become logically possible. We then begin to look for them in all possible anthropological nooks and crannies, and, sure enough, we are eventually rewarded. Incest is because of exchange, and the brother must step out to get a wife. No short cuts there!

This is why I believe that there is a lot of purchase in imagining variations. In this I am not only encouraged by Lévi-Strauss, but also by Edmund Husserl and his phenomenology. He too advocated that it was essential to undertake 'an imaginative variation of fact' if we wish to get to certitudes. In a way Lévi-Strauss too believes in the Husserlian dictum of 'bracketing away' the object of study, except that he does it differently.

Husserl's bracketing was an intuitive exercise to get to the essence of a phenomenon, its 'ideal'. Lévi-Strauss is too much of a Kantian to fall for that. His is not a search for essences but for phenomenal certitudes. If Lévi-Strauss encourages imagination, even intuition, they must result in *demonstrable* variations of relations. What he brackets away is matters of infrastructure which he heaps on Marx's table (Lévi-Strauss 1966: 130; 1968: 337). Lévi-Strauss's concern is only with the science of the superstructure, and nothing more. This allows him to roam freely from the Neolithic to the modern, from the bricoleur to the engineer, to demonstrate the fundamental unity of humankind (Lévi Strauss 1966: 13–15). Now at last we can answer the Husserlian question: why is it possible to teach geometry to a Papuan?

For Lévi-Strauss a study of potlatch is not just an exotic indulgence in a vestigial ceremony, but may actually tell us something about the European practice of exchanging wine. Such comparisons succeed in 'grasping the feelings, intentions and attitudes of natives involved in the cycle of prestations' (Lévi-Strauss 1968: 338). This is why Lévi-Strauss has argued that it is important 'to enlarge a specific experience to the dimension of a more general one, which thereby becomes accessible to men of another country or another epoch' (ibid.: 17).

Is the Context Contextualized? Beyond Binaries

This is the whole idea. How does one make familiar what seems strange and inexplicable to those who are far away. Instead of switching lenses, why not compare, as Lévi-Strauss advises? Instead of concentrating on an event why not be comparative and look for the structure? But that effort can get off the block only if we are convinced that the foreign is much nearer home than what the first glance would suggest.

Lévi-Strauss's comparative method dissolves strangeness by breaking down the exotic phenomenon into relations which can then be transformed. Once this is done we not only find unities between cultures, but also experience a sobering effect from the charge we get from the strange. Thus far I would happily follow Lévi-Strauss blindfolded.

After that we part ways. The relations I choose are my own, and not borrowed from Lévi-Strauss: the idea is but the content is not. To break down a phenomenon in terms of relations that are necessarily in binary opposition is restrictive. Lévi-Strauss accepts this limitation on some occasions too. In the Oedipus myth, for example, Jocaste's suicide has no structuralist consequence (ibid.: 216); nor is it necessary for the binary model that members of the turmeric totem be kept from consuming such an essential condiment (Lévi-Strauss 1966:126).

Also, why should we place everything on the structure of the human mind to remedy exotic tendencies in anthropology? Is it not enough to show that what seems unacceptable in one context is merely because the context in not properly understood? Instead of enquiring, as Lévi-Strauss does: 'Is the system systemic?' (Lévi-Strauss 1968: 48) one might equally ask: Is the context contextualized?

Inspired by Lévi-Strauss we can contextualize the context by interchanging positions that facts occupy in order to tease out their meaning. It is not as if the stop sign should always necessarily be red, but it is the relation that the three colours are in with respect to one another that allows for traffic management. As Lévi-Strauss himself suggests, if one were to change the colours around, or bring entirely different colours in their place, we could still make traffic signals work (ibid.: 94). In India, the coloured glass behind the lights is often missing, but by merely looking at the position of lights, a good driver will know what to do. Whether he abides by it or not, is another matter.

The important point, however, is that should we ever come across a semaphoring apparatus which is at odds with our experience then that should stimulate a search for a larger meaning. This must be a self-conscious exercise, for the spontaneous tendency in such circumstances is to issue dismissive judgements. Octavio Paz said somewhere in a clear Lévi-Straussian tone 'through writing we demolish things and turn them into meanings.' This position is significant as it sets out the need for writers, as much as for anthropologists, to think of human issues which rise above the here and now of the things they ostensibly write about. Thus while we may read about hopes and fears in an Indian village, it should be communicated such that somebody far away can make sense of the unfamiliar in familiar terms. True anthropologists, like true artists, belong to the world even as they are located in particular places and write about specific things. They are, after all, interested in the same thing: the concern is the Universal Man and not Men.

But caste is so unique! Does this one institution disrupt Lévi-Strauss's hard fought claims of unity? Moreover, it is not as if we are in some distant island, fenced by breezy palms and rolling seas. Caste is a quintessential Indian institution and involves a population that is second only to China, and not by much. India also thrusts itself to international notice by occupying a land mass so large that it is considered to be a sub-continent. If Lévi-Strauss falls here, and if India should then be a gigantic exception to his rule, then his inspirational worth is hugely devalued. But I believe Lévi-Strauss comes out stronger on account of the Indian example, though on the face of it, caste seems to defeat the whole idea of human unity, or universals.

Neutralizing the Exotic: Caste and Bunched Metaphors

Here we have a hierarchy of pollution and purity which is supposed to give everybody an unquestioned place at birth based on a ritual hierarchy. The Hindu urge to conform to this order is said to be so strong that Dumont believed it to be not just an ideology, which it is, but also a 'state of mind' (Dumont 1988: 24, 197). To make matters more difficult for human universalists, in the caste system even those at the bottom of the hierarchy actually believe they are polluted. This is why Moffat could argue that Hindu lower castes 'participate in their own subjugation' (Moffat 1979: 303).

This is surely the strangest form of stratification that the world has ever seen, or will hope to see. Not only are whole populations designated as polluting but the thus denigrated peoples find nothing wrong with it. They not only accept their lowly position, but also the reasoning that comes with it. It would, therefore, seem that the caste order readily 'brackets away' itself from all other forms of stratification. In which case, should Lévi-Straussian-inspired universalists pull down their shutters on this one unparalleled phenomenon? How can we dare dream now of fundamental unities, inter-subjectivities and, audaciously, of common horizons?

Caste does not just separate people from one another; it uses nature to mark out these divisions. As much as nature can be humanized (for example Grandville's sketch in Lévi-Strauss 1966: illustration 4), culture too can be naturalized as is the case with totemism. However, when Lévi-Strauss dispelled the totemic illusion, he did it in the context of equivalent homologies and not vertical hierarchies. Nevertheless, the principle that nature fixes cultural categories to discipline the cultural chaos in the mind, applies to caste as well.

We must remember that when castes rank Hindus in terms of being more or less pure, it is really a putative nature-based hierarchy. Hindus believe that there are substances, or bodily codes, which separate one caste from another, even though these diacritics are not visible to the naked eye (see Marriot and Inden 1977). It is for this reason castes erect barriers restricting marriage and sexual relations, as well as in matters of inter-dining. Should these boundaries be breached, pollution awaits one on the other side.

In this sense, caste hierarchically ranks nature, whereas totemism serializes it horizontally. Castes should then compete against other castes to claim affinity with a natural symbol that culture places on top. But if we go along with Dumont and Moffat, castes supposedly lower in the order should happily acquiesce to aligning themselves with lowly orders of nature. That would make caste ranking a vertical totemic sheet for there is an –the– board allegiance to the hierarchy. But this is not the case.

One early indication why Dumont's notion is incorrect is that in caste there is a paucity of claimed (not imputed) natural metaphors. This is because there is a crowding, or bunching, of metaphors with several castes claiming identity with the same proud beast. This must surely mean that there is trouble in the caste hierarchy and a dispute over relative positioning. Why else should there be so many claimants to the lion, tiger and other 'teeth bearing ancestors' (Lévi-Strauss 1966: 224)? If caste is totemism but read vertically, then unanimity should prevail on who gets which aspect of nature to call one's own.

Instead, there is a competition over metaphors for which reason, unlike totemism, castes do not need to summon the entire wealth of the natural world. The crowding, or bunching, of metaphors also explains why separations in the caste order are unbridgeable. Now we become aware that unlike what our elders told us, this Hindu hierarchy is a disputed one, else why should castes quarrel over metaphorical claims? If there is a choice between a cucumber and an ox, no caste would want to be a cucumber: an ox will always win. This logic works not just in the realm of sacrificial rituals (ibid.), but also explains the paucity of natural metaphors in the caste order.

In totemism, as Lévi-Strauss has shown, it is not humiliating for a group to be likened to a toad, cucumber or a reed of grass. This is because, unlike caste, totemism lays out nature horizontally and homologically. But it is so different when we encounter caste. Different castes position their identities angularly and when their relations unfold with the order they do not fold out to form an interdependent intellectual system. If totems are 'good to think' as Lévi-Strauss famously said, castes make it difficult to think together, but easier to quarrel. This is why, as Lévi-Strauss has noticed, castes are anti-solidarity in principle (ibid.: 116). Once this principle is accepted it does not really matter very much whether one is a Hindu, Muslim, Buddhist, Jain or Christian. Regardless of faith, caste succeeds in countering urges towards solidarity. No wonder Edmund Leach called caste a pan-Indian phenomenon (Leach 1969).

This paucity of natural symbols in the caste order is only so far as claimants are concerned. Nature is used much more generously, and testily, when it comes to attributing qualities to others. Accordingly, some castes consider other castes to be naturally dirty, timid, or lacking in clarity of thought, and, by the same token, valourize themselves for being fearless, entrepreneurial, hard working and intelligent. For each of these qualities they might also find a natural category that popularly represents those particular features. As claimant metaphors are so hotly contested, and attributional metaphors so lavishly unleashed, the tendency between castes is to drop gloves and slug it out in terms of pure natural abuse. Not always are these disputes displayed openly for want of political and economic resources, but symbolic rumbles can always be heard close to the ground.

Thus far we are more or less on what Lévi-Strauss said about caste. True he did not spell out why in the caste order there should be a competitive bunching of a few prized metaphors, or signifiers, but the suggestions are all there. In fact, when he discusses endogamy within a moiety, such as among the Chickasaw, the Creek or the Aranda, one can see parallels with caste quite clearly (Lévi-Strauss 1966: 118–19). This is why the basic proposition,

endogamy: exogamy : : hierarchy: egalitarianism holds.

And all this is there in Lévi-Strauss.

Why then do we need to be Lévi-Strauss-inspired to take the studies on castes further? Believe it or not, traffic lights show us the way.

IMAGINATIVE VARIATIONS: LEARNING FROM TRAFFIC LIGHTS

According to Dumont, the caste hierarchy is a pure hierarchy, untainted by considerations of power and wealth. This is why its ideology is so powerful that even lower castes accept their position within the system. For Dumont, and indeed, for the bulk of Indianists and Indologists, castes allow for just one hierarchy that places Brahmins on top and others in descending order of purity. But this ranking would appear less compelling if we take Lévi-Strauss's advice and conduct a few permutations. It would open up fresh possibilities, first logically and then empirically, and our understanding of caste may undergo a complete overhaul.

We need to recall here Lévi-Strauss's quick allusion to traffic lights (Lévi-Strauss 1964: 98ff). If the colours of traffic lights are altered or juggled around, the system can still remain secure. Likewise, it is possible to add, if castes are arranged like traffic lights, then a change in their relative positions would not disturb the system either. It would neither introduce solidarity, nor bring about a breakdown of the order. If this possibility is accepted then one is ready to look for alternative hierarchical formulations other than the 'pure one' that is traditionally posited. As history and particularly recent events demonstrate, subordinated castes have never been in happy subjugation. If they sat in sullen silence, it was always in wait for an opportunity to strike. When that happens, another hierarchy becomes regnant, another imagination gets realized. Lévi-Strauss has not commented on this aspect, but he could have. The ideas were there but perhaps they were far too wrapped up in binary opposites to allow for alternative kinds of transformations to show. If instead we move to the inspiration offered by traffic lights, a key conundrum can be solved.

Let us see how.

Any study of caste must gather within its sweep an understanding of how hierarchy and conflict are expressed in Indian society. This aspect was kept under wraps in most earlier works on caste for it was felt that the single hierarchy of purity with the Brahmin on top was all encompassing to allow for any disagreement in the ranks. It is not possible to be so sanguine any longer. Castes have fought as castes (let us leave aside the infrastructure for some time), and this would have been impossible if a single hierarchy reigned.

In fact, it was Leach who made the bold, and largely correct, suggestion that once castes compete with each other, the system is no more (Leach 1969). The consequences of this statement are far reaching and I am not sure if either Leach or his readers at that time saw all of them clearly. But what imagination does not do for you, history often accomplishes. Now we know that while the system is giving way in terms of occupation, power asymmetries, and so on, caste identities nevertheless persist. If truth be told, they are probably more forcefully expressed now than ever before.

If there are such heightened identities within each caste, why were they overlooked earlier? Why did generations of anthropologists not talk about these inherent caste tensions? Lévi-Strauss said that castes were not solidarity producing, but he did not say whence they got the armaments to go to war. Why indeed are caste identities so sharp and angular that it is even possible to talk in terms of 'caste patriotism'—so complete is the devotion to one's own community and background. So complete also is their animosity to their 'others'.

If such exhibitions of caste antagonism were not easily visible earlier then it is because of the infrastructure from which Lévi-Strauss carefully stayed away. In a closed natural economy of the village, vertical integration of the caste order is easy to uphold: patrons and clients know their place; there is the omnipresence of armed retainers and exploitation is based on 'extra-economic coercion'. Under these conditions to complain is to court certain pain. It may not always be the Brahmin who will inflict this injury; in fact, Brahmins are rarely capable of walking the talk and putting scriptural sanctions to work. In reality it was the 'dominant caste' that held sway (Srinivas 1987), but even that is not persuasive any more (Karanth 2004; Sahay 2004).

But now that the village economy is no longer closed, and not even natural, the much written about vertical integration is coming apart. It is estimated that over 45.5 per cent of Net Rural Domestic Income is non-agricultural. The infrastructure is changing and with it the relations between caste as well. As the earlier rural oligarch is more or less a blast that has past, small peasants are fighting with other small peasants and the landless in a more or less equal battle. As only equals can compete, for unequals either complain or get pulped, the ideology that provides symbolic energy for political battle must claim equality too. And sometimes more!

But how does this happen? Let us think of Lévi-Straussian transformations *sans* binary opposites; shall we say more in the spirit of the traffic lights? To oppose caste against totem in strict binary terms of exchange and exogamy is interesting, but not enough. Like traffic lights we must think instead of wholesale transfer of morphological positions from one ratchet to another. If the ordering of traffic lights can change without the system collapsing, then caste positions too can be altered to erect a new hierarchy. Like the old order, this too would be anti-solidarity in character.

This is a much closer approximation of Lévi-Strauss's spirit than what Dumont employed when he wrote *Homo Hierarchicus* (1988).

DUMONT'S HIERARCHY: STRUCTURALISM SANS TRANSFORMATION

Dumont had argued that his study of caste was a true structuralist one, but was it? Dumont believed that he was being structuralist because he placed the two poles of the hierarchy as radical inversions of each other. If the Brahmin is denoted by the + sign, the untouchable must get the − sign. If there is purity at one end, it must be absolute impurity at the other. Once we have these binary opposites in place our structuralist intentions cannot be questioned. So no matter what happens in the interstitial levels, the bookends of the Brahmin and untouchable keep castes properly stacked and in place.

But what happens to transformations? We know that from the very beginning Lévi-Strauss insisted that without transformations there was no structuralism. This is where Dumont made his big mistake. If he were pursuing a structuralist method then the empirical world is just one instance of the whole, and there could be many other logical possibilities which we should be able to imagine. Sometimes, when our minds tire at this exercise we can turn to anthropology and history for assistance as Husserl did when he wrote to Levy-Bruhl for help.

If Dumont had gone to history he would have found many instances of lower castes fighting their way to the throne, and even priesthood. If he had gone to anthropology, he would have found many tales of origin which dispute the Brahminical one that is appended to the *Rg Veda*. But Dumont chose to remain empiricist, and event bound, which is why his 'structuralism' is in doubt. He should have also remembered the structuralist axiom that whenever one is shortchanged by empirical instances there is always imagination to fall back on. The Brahminical version of the hierarchy is only one among several, real and imagined.

And if imagination does not play false, then there is that factual verification waiting to be found in the burning bushes. As in the ontological proof for the existence of God, if there is a word called perfect, and if we are all imperfect, then the word cannot be in vain. Therefore there must be God! This is how the eleventh-century St Anselm of Canterbury kept his pious faith alive. In some ways, structuralism too can strike a spiritual aura. Fortunately for anthropology, Lévi-Strauss's structuralism demands objective evidence at the end of the exercise.

Inspired by Lévi-Strauss it is possible to suggest that the priest need not always be on top, neither should a presently dominated untouchable caste accept its lowly position. But we must caution ourselves here and accept that binary transformations do not work out fully when we are considering and searching for other renditions of the caste hierarchy. But for such an imagination to take off we must rid ourselves of both primitive romanticism and despair. Therefore, while nobody is fundamentally good, and the poverty-equals-purity equation highly suspect, nobody accepts they are fundamentally bad either. This is the fundamental argument of *Tristes Tropiques* (Lévi-Strauss 1968: 334), and one which Lévi-Strauss never abandoned. In which case, by Lévi-Straussian lights, to believe that lower castes participate in their own subjugation is an analytical and empirical scandal. And so it is.

This comes to light once we start imagining different caste

hierarchies. A necessary premise for this to happen is to acknowledge that no caste acknowledges that it is fundamentally bad. In other words, the acceptance of untouchable or *shudra* status can only be enforced from outside, but never internalized. With this realization castes lose their exotic flavour, and our exercise in imagination can begin. Contrary to received literature, we must now open the doors to the possibility that like the rest of humankind, in the caste order too, no community willingly accepts its imputed impure status. A thoroughgoing permutation of the caste hierarchy demands such an assumption, or else it will not work at all.

Let us pick up the kaleidoscope that Lévi-Strauss handed to us in the 'Science of the Concrete' (Lévi-Strauss 1966). It appears that there are four elements with their associated qualities in the caste order whose relative positions can be altered internally without a systemic collapse. It is true that there are over 5000 endogamous castes, but in general the principle revolves around four categories.

Our first hierarchical arrangement is one where the Priest (*Brahmin*) occupies the highest position in the hierarchy, followed by the Warrior (*Kshatriya*), after whom comes the Merchant (*Vaishya*), and last of all the menials and helots (*Shudras*). This is the Brahminical hierarchy and it can be found appended to the *Rg Veda*, the first Hindu sacerdotal text. Though this vertical arrangement does not explicitly mention Untouchables, the slot is there to be occupied.

But this is just one origin tale.

There are many other origin tales that tell us different stories as if to aid our exercise in imagination. The leather workers (or *chamars*), who are designated as untouchables, believe that their origin is not a shameful one as described in traditional texts. In fact, their standard story is that they were Brahmins once but were downgraded by chicanery and deceit. But they are essentially still Brahmins (see Gupta 2000: 73–74). Other so-called untouchable castes, like the Doms, have similar narratives that depict their exalted origins (ibid.). There are several artisan castes too, like the Vanniyans, Kammalan, Barhai, and Lohar, who also claim Brahminical status (ibid.: 75).

But Brahmins are not always the aspirational model. Peasant castes, such as Jats (Chowdhry 2004), Yadavs (Michelutti 2004), Rajbhars (Sahay 2004) among many others, claim high status because they consider themselves to be Kshatriyas (or warriors). As Michelutti observes, the Yadavs trace their descent from Lord Krishna of the Mahabharata to give their herding profession a superior slant. Further they argue that as they were traditionally pastoral people, they are also natural politicians. Yadavs probably do not see much difference between herding cattle and herding people (Michelutti 2004).

Warrior status is claimed by a host of other castes too, both up and down what once appeared to be an unassailable hierarchy. The Kayasthas of Bengal, whom the Brahmins would place as number three in the pecking order, however argue that they are not only superior to the priestly castes, but actually employed them as cooks when they came out to the eastern provinces. In fact, their claim to Kshatriyadom is bolstered by their conviction that they once led an important mission from Kannauj to Bengal (Gupta 2000: 74–75). Mochis of Bombay province also claim Kshatriya status and so do the Chandraseni Kayastha Prabhu of Maharashtra. This ambition is also voiced among Shimpis (tailors), and the poor Kharwars of Bihar (ibid.).

This list is by no means complete. In fact, we should realize by now that no list is ever complete. One should not forget to add to our inventory those who put forward a kind of hyper-Brahmin status for they believe they are either children of gods, or incarnations of sacred things. Tamil bangle-makers assert that they were born out of the sacrificial fire. The Nhavis (traditional barbers) of Maharashtra say that they are the offspring of Nag Shesha, the serpent that garlands Lord Shiva's neck. The Kammalan caste traces its ancestry to Lord Vishwakarma, the architect of this universe (ibid.: 75)

There are some other interesting contestations to the Brahmin hierarchy that need to be considered. Many ex-untouchable castes state that as they were the autochthones of the Indic land mass, it is their culture that was the original one from which the other Hindu strains were derived. For example, the Meradha Kammara and Jajjagara Kamara (traditional blacksmiths) are proud to be *adis* because they are convinced that theirs was the first, and original, culture—a kind of mother board (Brouwer 1997: 71). The great lower caste social reformer, Jyotiba Phule, also advocated a similar view. According to him, Brahmins deceptively snatched the throne from Bali the beloved, pre-Aryan indigenous ruler and pushed them down (Gore 1993: 180). With the help of these origin claims not only are the so-called lower castes saying that they are superior to all others, but that latecomers such as Brahmins or Kshatriyas are plain, low born usurpers.

So we have the Brahmin model, the hyper-Brahmin model, the Warrior model, and the pre-Brahmin model. But why is the Merchant model missing? In fact, it is not, but it took me some time to imagine it before finding it. Even the merchants do not want to be Brahmins or Kshatriyas, but for reasons distinct from what the *adis* espouse. The merchants despise animal sacrificers and meat eaters for which reason they do not want to merge with Brahmin or Kshatriya caste templates (Babb 1998, Bayly 1983; Cort 2004). They are happy to stand apart from the rest as proud Vaishyas. They may have been rulers once, as the Agrawals claim (Babb 1998), but never Kshatriyas in spirit, substance or temperament—well, mostly substance. Not just that, merchants (or Baniyas) assert that they are purer than the rest because they are strict vegetarians and teetotalers (see also Bayly 1983: 379). Suborno Baniks (a merchant caste from Bengal) claim that they are the true Aryans as they walked over fire with Goddess Anayaka (Gupta and Bhasker n.d. 26; also Timberg 1978: 35). So there are merchants and merchants, but what unifies them is that they have a caste hierarchy of their own.

ORIGIN TALES: FROM IMAGINARY TO REAL VARIATIONS

Looking back at some of the origin tales mentioned, we can take some heart from Lévi-Strauss that while myths can be at the level of *langue* and *parole*, they can also be expressed as 'an absolute entity on a third level, which, though it remains linguistic by nature, is nevertheless distinct from the other two' (Lévi-Strauss 1968: 210).

These myths need not be looked at in terms of their internal structure, but as a whole in contrast to other myths of an identical discourse. In this process, what can also be observed is that these origin tales are written and re-written, handed down orally from generation to generation, or even switch gears from being once oral to now written (Narayan 2004: 2006), and yet the message remains the same in essence. 'Unlike poetry,' Lévi-Strauss said, 'the mythical value of myths survives the worst translations' (ibid.: 210).

So how should we now look at these origin myths? The first point is that the variations between different versions of the hierarchy are too remarkable to go unnoticed. The search for alternative expressions of the hierarchy was inspired by the Lévi-Straussian notion of transformations. Once the search for such variations began, instances kept pouring out. Besides the Brahmin, there were so many other versions of the hierarchy; some such as the *Adi* and the Merchant version came to notice because one went looking for them.

This does not mean that we have finally exhausted our stock of variations. There could be other versions too, but for that more imagination is required. But resting at this point of our imaginative journey let us take stock of what have we gathered so far. Like all myths, these myths too refer to events that had happened long ago, but they address issues of the day. Lévi-Strauss felt that myths help discuss unanswerable questions such as life, death and incest, but we can expand the repertoire further with the help of caste origin tales. These myths justify caste patriotism, strengthen caste identities, and help justify claims for upward mobility. They also satisfy clearly political motives which are interactional involving significant and general others. These myths are then not only internal ratiocinations about imponderables, as Lévi-Strauss said, but can also be seen as externalized projections of identity aimed at social positioning and political leverage.

What kind of variations are we then talking about?

Version I	Version II	Version III	Version IV
Brahmin	*Warrior*	*Merchant*	*Adi* (Hyper-Brahmin/ Before Aryan)
Warrior	*Brahmin*	*Brahmin*	*Brahmin or Kshatriya*
Merchant	*Merchant*	*Brahmin*	*Merchant*
Shudra	*Shudra*	*Shudra*	*Shudras*

The above is really a kaleidoscopic variation, or should we say a limited set of transformations as if the kaleidoscope had only four (perhaps, five) pieces. Or, if you wish, the above could be likened to a slightly expanded set of traffic lights. Notice there are no binary oppositions, but everything else is there. Unlike Dumont, no one hierarchy is privileged over the other. They are all logical equals of one another. This too is a characteristic of myth, once more, according to Lévi-Strauss.

At this point it is important to bring in the *infrastructure* once more. Far from being a hindrance, or extraneous to the discussion, changes in the infrastructure alert us to the possible variations in the hierarchy. Which version of the hierarchy will actually be expressed on the ground, and which versions will remain cloistered in low hamlets, depends upon who has wealth and power. The hierarchy that is broadcast and binding is the hierarchy of the powerful. It may be the Kshatriya version, or the Brahmin, or even the Baniya (merchant) variety. All these versions have been expressed at one time or another.

In the case of the Merchant model we need to quickly consider the case of the Vahivanca Barot flip flop (see Shah and Shroff 1973). This is a caste of bards who earlier served the princes of North Gujarat and therefore called themselves Kshatriyas in emulation. In the fullness of time, in post-Independence India, merchants and not Kshatriyas began to dominate Gujarat. So the Barots now call themselves Kapol Banias (a merchant caste).

But let us take a close look at Version IV. This version of the hierarchy is usually one that is associated with low castes, even untouchables. Today this hierarchy can be openly expressed as the control of the landed castes has more or less slipped away in the villages. Democracy and urbanization have freed these landless ex-untouchables from the patron-clients to whom they were bound. True, the *Adi* version is not burnished as highly as the others are, but it parades in equal splendour on the streets against its many contenders.

There is, however, an interesting matter of detail in the hierarchy of the *Adi*. Why is the category of shudra still there? Should not the untouchables resist the very category, altogether? But if it can be logically posited as it has been in the above hierarchy, then perhaps it can also be empirically possible. Indeed, it is. I.P. Desai has shown that the so-called untouchable castes may dispute their position in the hierarchy, but they do not necessarily believe that others should not occupy that slot.

For this reason, Desai argued that the phenomenon of 'untouchability among untouchables' should not be overlooked (Desai 1976). One sees this in a number of contexts: in Maharashtra between Mahars and Mangs, Matangs or Chamars; in Uttar Pradesh between Valmikis and Harijans; in Tamilnadu between Pariyars and Pallars; in Karnataka between Lambankis, Oddas, Koramas, Holeyas and Madigas (Karanth 2004: 144–45; 149, and *passim*), and so on.

TRANSMORPHING RIDDLES

A purist undertaking of structuralism would object to the above schema. These are not typical transformations as signs are not being exchanged, but whole bodies are. To argue that only the signs at the extremes matter, but not the interstitial levels, as Dumont does, is not satisfying for there are great quarrels between different levels as to who should be placed where. If the term 'transformation' is objectionable, then perhaps we should think in terms of 'transmorphation'. It will be hard, even misleading to understand the various versions of the hierarchy in terms of binary opposites. Instead of signs transforming we have substances trans-morphing.

Even if we were to coin the neologism 'trans-morph' instead of transform, there is no doubt that the inspiration for this has come to me from Lévi-Strauss. It is Lévi-Strauss who taught us in brilliant prose that unless we see alternative possibilities of that which is given and favoured, we will be insensitive to other logical equals. The origin tales are logical equals, and they all see themselves as possessing an exalted past. What virtues they value differ from version to version, but they are equally plausible, or equally fantastic, depending on one's angle of vision.

Such an approach solves three abiding anthropological puzzles, one that has been spoken of widely, and the other kept *sotto voce*, and the third mentioned by Lévi-Strauss without fully resolving it. The first refers to the argument that members of lower castes willingly accept their subjugated position, and is this not unique? Hence, the recourse to the Hindu state of mind that primed generations of exotic-favouring anthropologists. But once the Dumontian hierarchy was suspected of being incorrectly structuralist, other variations of the hierarchy were sought, and found.

These transformations, or trans-morphations, if you will, show very clearly that no caste actually accepts their degraded status. Without leaving the caste order, and without even distancing themselves from the principle of biological substances, members of the so-called lower castes put forward alternate hierarchies that place them on top. If this was not appreciated in the past then it is probably because Lévi-Strauss had not inspired Indologists enough. To dispute one's status in a hierarchy does not necessarily mean to discard the ideology behind this order, or the ontology that this epistemology forwards.

This is why many lower caste anti-Brahmin movements have not disputed the theory behind caste rankings as such, except their own position within it. If castes can fight for superiority, though not always successfully, then the Hindu system of stratification loses its exotic appeal. It is now quite like other ascriptive rivalries, though the gradations here are finer and more obsessive. That is why we should always designate certain castes as low or high by putting these adjectives in quotation marks.

The other riddle, which was never spoken about loudly, is also resolved thanks to the capacity for hierarchies to trans-morph. We now understand why caste identities do not have to collapse when castes start competing against one another. Though every hierarchy tries to sublate and deny other hierarchies, the truth is that these alternate expressions are out there, sometime in a subterranean fashion. When we talk of caste wars it is also an epistemological struggle between hierarchies.

Now to the last, and perhaps the most intractable puzzle of all.

THE BARBER AND THE BRAHMIN

In his scrutiny of caste Lévi-Strauss asks: '(W)ho would shave the barber (Lévi-Strauss 1966: 126)?' The answer he gives is partly evasive. According to him as there are always more barbers and potters than an economy needs, each caste is compelled to be 'partly endofunctional' (ibid.: 122, 126). In other words, we should not be too rigid in the business of occupational specialization. There must always be room to maneouvre.

Given the firmness with which Lévi-Strauss resolves most issues, this is certainly out of character. The reason why Lévi-Strauss takes this uncertain step is because he stops at the barber. He should have gone on to ask: Who will pray for the Brahmin? Once this question is raised, the answer can be found in the trans-morphed hierarchies we have just encountered. What makes these alternative hierarchies meaningful and context-laden is that they speak to each other. They all agree on the question of bodily substances separating members of different castes such that if a cucumber claims to be an ox, other certified oxen would object.

First, the barber and the priest face these problematic choices only during moments of high ritual noon. A barber is needed for a tonsure to signify the end of the mourning period for the male descendants of the deceased. A marriage, or ritual purification, is also an occasion when a Brahmin must call upon some other priest to officiate. Only on such occasions do the barber and the priest face a dilemma. On an everyday basis, most people shave themselves and most priests pray in their own homes.

As an aside, it must also be mentioned that rendering services, even that of a Brahmin, lowers the service provider in relation to the service receiver. This is why in traditional societies if one was a landlord then one received services and rendered only patron-like munificence, depending upon the whim of the day.

The first step towards solving the barber and the priest dilemma is then to see disputes within caste clusters as replays of what happens between caste clusters. As there are constant altercations among different Brahmin *jatis* (the endogamous unit) as to who is superior to whom, it is almost impossible for a Brahmin to find a priest other than from within his caste to render him services. If a Brahmin from a different *jati* agrees to do it then he is willingly becoming a service provider—or a cucumber to somebody else's ox. The same logic holds for barbers as well. So if we take the logic of hierarchies trans-morphing further we will find that between different castes of Brahmins there is no sense of equality either. Myths and counter myths prevail to prove the superiority or inferiority of other Brahmans.

Members of a Brahmin *jati* will consider other Brahmins to be lower than them, and perhaps not Brahmins of any description. Recall the various Brahmin myths that were related earlier. In fact, the status of some Brahmins, such as the Maha-Brahmins, who officiate at funerary service, is almost that of a Shudra. Needless to say, Maha-Brahmins do not feel that way at all.

Once these ranks are trans-morphed what comes through is that the position of the Brahmin becomes a bit of a fiction. Anyone who renders priestly services is a priest. The Lingayats of Mysore have their own priests, so do some leather workers, and palanquin bearers (see Gupta 2000: 117). In fact, there are Brahmins who would also perform ritual ceremonies for Bhars, Pasis and Dosadhs—castes that were once considered below the pollution barrier (ibid.). If one bears in mind that service providers are below service receivers then the validity of trans-morphing the so-called intra-Brahmin hierarchy becomes clear.

There are Brahmins, such as the Bhumihars and Babbhans of Bihar, the Anavils of Gujarat, or the Jhas of Bihar, who are, in a manner of speaking, Kshatriya Brahmins. Bhumihars, Jhas and

Anavils do not perform rituals themselves for they consider it to be demeaning. They would not marry into families of professional priests either—so strong is the distinction between service providers and service receivers. The priest who will perform rituals for such families must come from a designated Brahmin service giver. This problem is not difficult to resolve as Kshatriya Brahmins always functioned with a retinue of service class priests.

But what about a performing, or practising, Brahmin? Who will pray for him? Against this background, the only person who will pray for such a Brahmin is a clan member, and the only one who will shave the barber will have to be of the same ritual status of the barber. They cannot even go to their wives' family or to their daughter-in-law's family for such services even though a bride taker is superior to a bride giver. The complication is that even though with the gift of the virgin, or *kanyadaan*, the bride givers accept a lower status than the bride takers, nevertheless they both belong to the same caste. In terms of purity of bodily substances, they are equals. If they were to perform services for the bride takers then it would mean that they belong to a different caste and this would offend endogamy. Besides, once the daughter gives birth to a male child she becomes a bride taker herself and the statuses of the two families are neutralized.

Endogamy and exopraxis forces this crisis on ritual occasions because it is not easy to find a suitable inferior by consensus. When hierarchies are in dispute, and this holds within caste clusters as well as between caste clusters, then on significant ritual occasions, castes have no option but to convert exopraxis to the level of autopraxis. From the outside they may all look like Brahmins or Barbers, and even behave as one, but within the caste cluster of Brahmin, Barber (warrior or merchant) there are disputed and fractious hierarchies. Had different Brahmin *jatis* and different Barber *jatis* been aligned in a consensual hierarchy, this problem would not have arisen at all.

But then the Lévi-Straussian impetus to move from transforming signs to trans-morphing hierarchies would not have been evident either. The riddle of the barber and the priest would have not appeared so puzzling if Lévi-Strauss were to take that further step and trans-morph categories and substances. This would still be in keeping with the Lévi-Straussian dictum of studying Man and not men in order to assert the fundamental of human kind. A phenomenon that once appeared unique is now familiar, without being the same as any other.

If we have come this far in taking the exotica out of castes, then it is almost entirely due to the inspiration I have drawn from Lévi-Strauss. It should not really matter that this presentation does not look truly structuralist, as long as something useful has been said. We all have our favourite Lévi-Strauss: some of us transform, others trans-morph. What unites us in our admiration of the savant is his dictum to distrust any empirical manifestation of a phenomenon as the ultimate one.

References

Babb, L.A. 1998. 'Rejecting Violence: Sacrifice and the Social Identity of Trading Communities', *Contributions to Indian Sociology*, (n.s.) vol. 32: 387–407.

Bayly, C.A. 1983. *Rulers, Townsmen and Bazaars: North Indian Society in the Age of British Expansion, 1770–1870*. Cambridge: Cambridge University Press.

Brouwer, Jan. 1997. 'The Goddess for Development: Indigenous Economic Concepts Among South Indian Artisans', *Social Anthropology*, vol. V: 69–82.

Cort, John E. 2004. 'Jains, Caste and Hierarchy in North Gujarat', in Dipankar Gupta, ed., *Caste in Question: Identity or Hierarchy?* New Delhi: Sage Publications.

Desai, I.P. 1976. *Untouchability in Rural Gujarat*. Mumbai: Popular Prakashan.

Dumont, Louis. 1988. *Homo Hierarchicus: The Caste System and its Implications*. London: Weidenfeld and Nicholson.

Gore, M.S. 1993. 'Social Movement and the Paradigm of Functional Analysis: With Reference to the Non-Brahman Movement in Maharashtra', in Yogesh Atal, ed., *Understanding Indian Society: Festschrift in Honour of S.C. Dube*. Delhi: Har-Anand Publication.

Gupta, Dipankar. 2000. *Interrogating Caste: Understanding Hierarchy and Difference in Indian Society*. New Delhi: Penguin.

Gupta, Dwarkanath C. and S. Bhasker. n.d. *Vyasas: A Sociological Study*. New Delhi: Ashish Publishing House.

Husserl, Edmund. Origin of Geometry.

Karanth, Gopal. 2004. 'Replication or Dissent? Culture and Institutions among Scheduled Castes in Karnataka', in Dipankar Gupta, ed., *Caste in Question: Identity or Hierarchy?* New Delhi: Sage Publications.

Leach, Edmund. 1969. 'Introduction', in Edmund R. Leach, ed., *Aspects of Caste in South Asia, Ceylon and Northwest Pakistan*. Cambridge: Cambridge University Press.

Lévi-Strauss, Claude. 1962. *Totemism*. Boston: Beacon Press.

——— 1966. *The Savage Mind*. Chicago: University of Chicago Press.

——— 1968. *Structural Anthropology*. Harmondsworth: Penguin.

Marriot, McKim and Ronald Inden. 1977. 'Towards an Ethnosociology of the South Asian Caste System', in Kenneth A. David, ed., *The New Wind: Changing Identities in South Asia*. Chicago: Aldine Publications.

Moffat, Michael. 1979. *An Untouchable Community in South India: Structure and Consensus*. New Jersey: Princeton University Press.

Narayan Badri. 2004. 'Inventing Caste History: Dalit Mobilisation and Nationalist Past', in Dipankar Gupta, ed., *Caste in Question: Identity or Hierarchy?* New Delhi: Sage Publications.

Sahay, Gaurang. 2004. 'Hierarchy, Difference and the Caste System: A Study of Rural Bihar', in Dipankar Gupta, ed., *Caste in Question: Identity or Hierarchy?* New Delhi: Sage Publications.

Shah, A.M. and G. Shroff. 1975. 'The Vahivanca Barots of Gujarat: A Caste of Genealogists and Mythographers', in Milton Singer, ed., *Traditional India: Structure and Change*. Jaipur: Rawat Publications.

Srinivas, M.N. 1987. *Dominant Caste and Other Essays*. Delhi: Oxford University Press.

Timberg, Thomas A. 1978. *The Marwaris: From Traders to Industrialists*. Delhi: Vikas Publishing House.

Why a Cousin Becomes a Spouse
Elementary, says Lévi-Strauss

Rita Brara

As an intellectual and an anthropologist, Lévi-Strauss is without an equal—non-pareil as you would say it in French. Like a great explorer, the scale of his endeavours impressively traverses vast cultural and geographical swathes and simultaneously he zooms in, in the manner of a detective, on precise, local details. He continues to dazzle students with the extraordinary boldness and clarity of his ventures as they make their first forays into anthropology and, especially, I think, in the study of kinship.

All along he builds on the contributions of earlier anthropologists, affirming that anthropology is, indeed, an empirical discipline. Indeed, there is need to reiterate the grounding of his contributions in empirical bedrock because that is often eclipsed in discussions of his structuralist method. From his enquiry into the corpus of empirical studies in the field of kinship, he discerns a pattern in complex and bewildering kinship terminologies as well as marriage practices.

What gives rise to the pattern on the ground is in his view a structure—a structure of exchange and reciprocity that he seeks to unravel. By relating the kinship terminology of a people to their rules of descent, residence and marriage, he shows an underlying logic that is indeed elementary. From his exegesis of kinship patterns ranging from Siberia to Australia, he propounds the thesis that it is indeed, the giving and taking of women in marriage, or in one word, exchange, that constitutes the means of integration among human beings and the marriage of cousins is its simplest expression.

What Lévi-Strauss offers, then, is an unusual feast for kinship die-hards—a storyline that unravels as he works his way from distant to proximate cultures through the patient perusal of the work of his forebears. He develops a logical method to analyse and synthesize kinship facts and delivers, in my view, the most convincing analysis of cross-cousin marriage across the cultures that he investigates. In *Elementary Structures* (1969) especially, he does not just concentrate on expounding what in almost banal terms is referred to as the structuralist method but gives us a rich harvest—a yield so extraordinary that we continue to dip into it even today.

Lévi-Strauss's (1969) elementary structure of kinship has a dual aspect—incest prohibitions that indicate who not to marry, and a positive rule that broadly defines who to marry. By contrast, complex structures focus on incest prohibitions alone. He shows how kin-classifications that club siblings and parallel cousins, while distinguishing cross-cousins, go hand-in-hand with a rule that specifies the marriage class into which an ego should marry or identifies the type of relationship that enables one to determine marriageable cousins (bilateral cross-cousins, and matrilateral or patrilateral cross-cousins). And then, armed with this insight, he cuts through the thicket of diverse kinship terminologies with unrelenting logic and systematization

What follows is for the kinship die-hards only. With dual organization, you have two marriage classes—A marries B, B marries A. It can co-exist with any rule of descent and any rule of residence. The 3-class system is attested by the Karidjeri, for instance. Move onto four classes and look at whether the rule of residence and the rule of descent run in the same direction—what he calls harmonic—or different directions, that is to say, disharmonic. Making the most of the divergence of residence and descent rules, disharmonic regimes place children in classes other than those of their parents, thus he explains the 4-class Kareira system, the 8-class Aranda system, and indeed any other system based on an even number of classes. These disharmonic kinship systems, in his view, are characterized by bilateral cross-cousin marriage, direct or restricted exchange and continuous reciprocity integrating all the groups in that society.

A different underlying logic works 4-class systems that are harmonic. Where the principle of descent and the principle of residence are tied together, that is to say, you have patrilineal descent/ patrilocal residence or matrilineal descent/matrilocal residence, an added dimension promotes societal integration between groups. This additional dimension is the idea of directionality in the marriage of cousins, or what is called unilaterality—A marries B, B marries C, C marries D, D marries E and so on, but not vice-versa. By contrast with disharmonic regimes, harmonic regimes are characterized by unilateral cross-cousin marriage, (either patri or matri), indirect or generalized exchange but here, too, different consequences materialize depending on whether you marry the matrilateral cross-cousin (MBD) or the patrilateral cross-cousin (the FZD). In Lévi-Strauss's view, it is only marriage with the bilateral cousin or the matrilateral cross-cousin that gives you the capacity to forge links with an indefinite number of groups and over generations, that is to say, a global integration across groups. By contrast, marriage with the patrilateral cross-cousin is what Lévi-Strauss refers to as the ungenerous Cheap-Jack of marriage arrangements. Here a family can only wait to claim the sister's daughter in marriage for a generation or scarcely stay away even that long. In a modification of marriage with the FZD, the ZD is claimed even earlier—as in MyB- eZD marriages. Although patrilateral cross-cousin marriage falls in the category of unilateral marriage and indirect exchange, it is closer to the pole of restricted exchange. As a procedure, it segments the society into groups by following 'return' marriages within a system of generalized exchange, rather than a valuable form of integration.

Lévi-Strauss cracked the harmonic regimes only after analysing the Murngin kinship system where a 4-class harmonic regime alternated with an 8-class system in the following generation. Almost like piecing a jigsaw puzzle together, he showed how the principle of generalized exchange in a 4-class harmonic regime lay buried as a deep structure until it was excavated.

So what underlies these elementary structures of kinship or why a cross-cousin becomes a spouse is the practice of exchange between groups of men. The giving and taking of wives in marriage is an expression of reciprocity, and ongoing exchange works as societal glue. Was there a way out of this recurrent pattern? For the most part, as he puts it, that possibility was denied to social man. A world where you could keep your daughters to yourself could be conjured only in myths, though somewhat speculatively, Lévi-Strauss investigates the transition to complex structures.

On the one hand, he notes that the Crow-Omaha system forms a sort of halfway house between elementary and complex structures. On the other, he ventures to suggest that the dilemma of who the king's daughter would marry breaks the logic of generalized exchange at the pinnacle of the feudal hierarchy. It is epitomized, for instance, in the rite of *swayamvara* where the groom is chosen by proving his merit. In Lévi-Strauss' reckoning here was a presaging of complex structures of kinship that connects Europe and Asia, apparent in the individualization of the marriage contract, the equality of partners in the marriage vows and the ostensible bridging of the social status between the king's family and his son-in-law that is based on the merit of the groom.

KINSHIP AND MARRIAGE IN INDIA:
STILL DIPPING INTO LÉVI-STRAUSS' FOUNTAINHEAD

Louis Dumont (1957) was perhaps the first to enrich his own theoretical orientation by drawing upon Lévi-Strauss for developing his insights into kinship in India. He persuasively argues for the recognition of the marriage alliance as a principle for the apprehension of kinship and marriage practices in South India, an aspect that is reflected in terminology and transmitted over generations. Lévi-Strauss had, of course, laid its contours in *Elementary Structures*. And Dumont (1957) extends and refines this line of thinking, finding evidence for what he terms an alliance perspective in gift-giving practices, rites of passage and kinship terminology.

In comparing Lévi-Strauss and Dumont's studies on marriage, I notice both continuities and subtle shifts in vocabulary and analysis. Dumont moves away from the use of the term 'exchange' and prefers the term 'alliance' in order to characterize marriage arrangements in South India. That the term 'alliance' continues to resonate in current anthropology is perhaps because it better captures the sense of reciprocity between groups of men who exchange women. Yet, the significance of the difference between restricted exchange and generalized exchange, in my view, continues to be useful for the study of India. The Indian civilization has consistently distinguished barter or overtly exchangist marriages that form part of direct or restricted exchange from marriages that are in consonance with generalized exchange expressed in the ideal of *kanyadaan* or the gift of the daughter, which will not brook a direct return.

While Lévi-Strauss brings out the structural differences and commonalities between matrilateral, patrilateral and bilateral cross-cousin marriage, again, Dumont does not consider the bilateral modalities of cousin marriage in his studies of South India. But more recently, Thomas Trautmann (1981) has drawn upon and refined some of Lévi-Strauss' earlier theses. What, Trautmann asks, is the principle by which we can explain a preference for the unilateral cross-cousin from a kinship terminology that expresses bilateral cross-cousin marriage? And within the class of unilateral cousins, when should we expect to find a preference for the patrilateral or the matrilateral cousin? Trautmann's (ibid.) search takes him back to the Hindu Dharmashastras and the Indian notion of *kanyadaan*.

In his study of the Dravidian region, Trautmann finds the prominence of the matrilateral cross-cousin marriage, in fact, in the practice of the Brahmins who were the most influenced by the ideals of the Dharmashastras. Trautmann concludes that this unilateral form of cross-cousin marriage in the south Dravidian area, especially, is derived, historically speaking, from bilateral cross-cousin marriage in the region. While the lower castes go in for patrilateral cross-cousin marriage that entails a return of the woman, as it were, tribes such as the Maria Gonds in the central Dravidian region in India still practise marriage with the bilateral cross-cousin and its variants.

I am highlighting the contributions made by Louis Dumont and Thomas Trautmann here with a motive. First, to argue that these later researches into kinship in India would not have arisen unless the field had been readied by Lévi-Strauss's pioneering studies of marital exchange. Once formulated, kinship studies could explore dimensions of cousin marriage and alliance that had not come to the fore earlier though now of course we take it for granted that delving into marriage exchange and alliance, along with descent, helps us to apprehend kinship and marriage patterns.

Yet, both Dumont and Trautmann, like Lévi-Strauss before

them, focus in the main on Hindu marriage, leaving out of their purview cousin marriage among Muslims in north and south India. Cousin marriage among Muslims is steadfastly kept out of the framework making it seem as if Muslim groups were not part and parcel of India as a historical becoming. The understanding of hybrid religious practices and cousin marriages among Muslims, I think, is significant for an understanding of marriage patterns in India both synchronically and over time.

MUSLIM MARRIAGES IN INDIA: BOTH PARALLEL AND CROSS COUSINS CAN BE SPOUSES

What is described in anthropological parlance as parallel cousin marriage has been alluded to as the 'black box' in Lévi-Strauss's theory of kinship. He leaves it out of his reckoning but no one mind, not even Lévi-Strauss's, can process it all. In making the rationale underlying cross-cousin marriage visible, Lévi-Strauss singles out and privileges the B-Z relationship. This relationship in his view enables a structure of exchange to be built up based upon the credit and debit of women. While he approvingly cites the Wintu's depiction of the B-Z relationship as 'the beautiful one' in support of cross-cousin marriage, B-B and Z-Z relationships that lead to parallel cousin marriage are left out. He treats parallel cousin marriage as a modality that facilitates class endogamy that is prevalent in Iran and Iraq, and the matter rests there.

A seminal paper by Veena Das in 1971, titled the 'Structure of Marriage Preferences among Urdu-speakers in West Pakistan', was the first to consider parallel cousin marriage among Muslims from a Lévi-Straussian perspective. As Das (1971) puts it, the marriage of cousins here stems from the relationship between siblings and their spouses—those who have a right to bestow their children and those who have a right to claim them. While she notes that the divide between cross and parallel cousins is not 'intrinsic' to their system, she infers that the choice of a particular bride or groom is structured beyond the identification of marriage classes, in that the children of siblings are preferred to the children of those who are the parents' cousins at this level. From her point of view, however, it is important to distinguish between marriage strategies that make for the exclusiveness of groups exemplified by marriage within the *khandaan* (a term for family) and marriage strategies that make for alliance, exemplified by cross-cousin marriage in South India, for instance. She also notes that the direct exchange of son-daughter sets in marriage between families is eschewed.

In the period following Lévi-Strauss's work, anthropologists such as Pierre Bourdieu too, refrained from 'typing' cousin marriages, increasingly cognizant of the social and economic histories that shape these matrimonial strategies. The realization that what was classed as a distinct form of cousin marriage could grow out of diverse micro-familial politics and constellations is now widely accepted. Yet, what holds my attention are two unresolved issues—one pertaining to religious injunctions that either allow or disallow cousin marriages and the other to the boundedness of the domain of kinship as it were—which I shall discuss by drawing on my fieldwork among Muslims in the former princely state of Malerkotla in north India. The two groups that I focus on are the chief's lineage known as the Afghan Sherwanis and a group of peasants called Muslim Kambohs who are primarily vegetable-growers in this region.

What are locally interpreted as religion-influenced preferences, for or against cousin marriages, continue to influence people. The incest taboos that define whom you cannot marry (which cousins to exclude or include), based on religious injunctions, still tell us much about the structure of marriage proscriptions and practices. As is well known, the closest marriageable relatives among Muslims include both patrilateral and matrilateral parallel and cross-cousins.

Although religious injunctions that determine incest prohibition suggest and permit cousin marriage among Muslims in their altered contexts, in contrast with their northern Hindu pasts where such marriages were forbidden.

Second, among Muslims, cousin marriages of both cross and parallel modalities exist alongside marriages with non-relatives, if I stay with extant anthropological categories as descriptive terms. In other words, where the distinction between cross and parallel cousins is not made, cousin marriages of four types FBD, FZD, MBD, MZD – stemming from B-B, B-Z, Z-Z ties are recognized in categories marked by peoples.

While studying the marriage practices of the inhabitants of the former Muslim princely state of Malerkotla, I found that both former Muslim rulers and peasants permitted cousin marriage of these four modalities, considered from a synchronic vantage point. What anthropologists describe as the marriage of cousins, was viewed as marriage with the children of four types of relatives – FB, FZ, MB, MZ – 'real' (*sage*) relatives being distinguished from classificatory ones, in the main. Here the kinship terminology denoted all four types of cousins as brothers or sisters by specifying the relationship to Ego with reference to the connecting relative – as in FBS (*tayazad* or *chachazad bhai/ behan*) MBS (*mamazad bhai/ behan*) and any one could become a spouse. But the pattern of cousin choices diverged among Muslim groups on the ground.

As a marriage strategy, marriage with the patrilateral parallel cousin was especially espoused in contracting the first marriage of a ruler. The Afghan chiefs at Malerkotla over four generations first married their FBDs after 1857 though historical records reveal that they had formerly sought matrimonial allies outside the state. The 'pure' and 'honourable' status of marriage with the FBD was offered as the reason for this later preference; after all, it conformed to the marriage favoured by the Prophet Muhammad for his own daughter. This practice also seemed to support an exclusive line within the *biradiri* or fraternity of Afghan Sherwanis at Malerkotla. However, since the rulers married polygamously, their subsequent marriages were with an MBD and/or an FZD who often belonged to another princely state. Marriage with the MZD, though permitted, was less frequent.

The rulers' daughters/sisters were either married to the rulers of other Afghan states, either FZSs or MBSs, or with scions of other named *khandaans* or branches of the Afghan Sherwanis at Malerkotla, who were real or classificatory FBSs. Marriages with the FZDs or MBDs outside Malerkotla evidently created marriage alliances integrating different Afghan clans. However, marriage with a distant or classificatory FBS also re-integrated segments within the ruling patrilineage by drawing distant agnates into the fold through a marriage alliance. The view that valuable alliances were established through marriage with the patrilateral parallel cousin did not hold here. The view 'We marry our enemies', resonated among Malerkotla's ruling Afghans who believed that by giving a daughter in marriage, you gained an ally. While the Afghans averred that everyone who shared the patronymic clan name was related, exclusivity was asserted most actively by pursuing marriages that brought you closer to the ruler's line.

The distinct modalities of real and classificatory cousin marriage facilitated the simultaneous perusal of exclusiveness and alliance both within the *biradiri* or fraternity and outside it. But the exchange of son-daughter sets between two siblings was not practised in keeping with the distinction between wife-receivers and wife-givers that was followed by Hindu elites.

By contrast with the former rulers, the Muslim Kamboh peasants of Malerkotla who were more recent converts to Islam, favoured cross-cousin marriage, eschewing marriage with the patrilateral parallel cousin altogether. The Kambohs were divided into *gots* or exogamous patrilineal groups – what Lévi-Strauss calls 'the little gotras'. They refrained from using the term *khandaan* for their families since it connoted upper classness. A group that shared the same *got*, transmitted as a patronymic, was assumed to have descended from a common ancestor and believed to share in a relationship of the body (*jism ka rishta*) that precluded marriage under their former Hindu injunctions. However, new incest prohibitions with the changeover to Islam were gradually incorporated in a group-specific idiom. Marriage with cross-cousins here was allowed since these cousins belonged to different *gots* or patrilineal clans. Kamboh marriages frequently included non-cousins as well but their incest prohibitions and marriage practices were a hybrid of Muslim and Hindu marriage mores.

Further, the Kambohs distinguished *'pun'* marriages (wherein you give a daughter in marriage to unrelated Kambohs) from *'batta'* marriages (that were characterized by the direct exchange of a son-daughter set with another son-daughter set). The word *'pun'* derived from *'punya'* or religious merit that was thought to be attained when a father gave a daughter to a family without the expectation of a return, as with the Hindu *kanyadaan* (the gift of a daughter in marriage). As an emic model of direct and indirect exchange, the structure of *batta* and *pun* marriages corresponds very closely, I think, to Lévi-Strauss's etic categories of restricted and generalized exchange.

Yet, in the Kamboh reckoning, the connotations of exchangist marriage were reserved for marriages by direct exchange or *batta*. These *batta* marriages did not meet with the approval that was reserved for *pun* marriages to unrelated Kambohs – that is to say, marriages contracted by indirect exchange. An expression of marriage by indirect exchange sign-posted the family's credit among the Kambohs in kinship and economic terms in contrast to the economic and social poverty of marriage by barter.

Through this account I have tried to show, first, that cousin marriages are apparently moored in the local histories of different social groups—economic, political, religious—but both patrilateral and matrilateral parallel and cross-cousins formed the matrix from which a spouse was chosen. Reviewing the elementary structure of marriage relationships at Malerkotla, it becomes apparent that the relationship of a B-Z pair is not especially privileged. While Lévi-Strauss leaves parallel cousin marriages out of his purview, it seems to me that the understanding of these excluded cousin marriages, too, benefits from an alliance perspective. Where incest taboos do not proscribe it, parallel and cross-cousins can be included within a single frame.

If the B-B as well as the Z-Z relationships are brought into the reckoning of cousin marriage as well, within the expanded terms of discourse, then marriage with the patrilateral parallel cousin and the matrilateral parallel cousin do not appear as a sort of heresy in the marriage alliance framework. A principle that Lévi-Strauss propounds most emphatically in his work on totemism, in fact, suggests that one must exhaust all the terms in a universe of discourse before setting up a table of possibilities that excludes some cousins and includes others. Further, while in Lévi-Strauss's reckoning, classificatory cousins are drawn into the division of marriageable and non-marriageable classes, at Malerkotla, like in West Pakistan, 'real' cousins are preferred over classificatory cousins.

At Malerkotla, cousin marriage practices were religious hybrids evolving in relation to past and present incest injunctions which interest anthropologists engaged in comparisons of marriages across space or within the same society. But religious proscriptions and prescriptions, too, are altered in the direction of fundamentalist, heterodox or value-neutral interpretations of cousin marriage, and such alterations are revealed in a people's preferences, seen synchronically. On the other hand, diachronic studies bring out the direction of change in cousin marriage practices and preferences in relation to a group's own marriage arrangements in the past.

To abstract structure from practices prevalent in geographical and cultural spaces that lie outside the chosen area of Lévi-Strauss's own study, in my view, is to take Lévi-Strauss's analyses of marriage exchange and cousin marriage forward by facilitating a comparative study. To elucidate the different modalities of cousin marriage and incest prohibitions evident among peoples of diverse religious traditions such as Islam, Judaism and Christianity and their hybrids, in the present, may need us to go beyond the structures that Lévi-Strauss delineated in his masterly analysis of cross-cousin marriage.

As anthropologists from non-western cultures begin to compare marriage practices across societies on the same plane, it becomes apparent that cousin marriage straddles both western and non-western societies though its meaning, function and cultural context varies. I might mention at this point that two of the pioneers in the anthropology of kinship and marriage—Lewis Henry Morgan and Claude Lévi-Strauss—both had a first-hand acquaintance with cousin marriage. In his book on 'Lewis Henry Morgan and the Invention of Kinship', Trautmann (1987) notes that Morgan was married to a first cousin. He suggests that perhaps Morgan could not connect Dravidian terminologies with the rule of cross-marriage because that would have made his own marriage appear primitive. Only recently I learned that Lévi-Strauss was no stranger to cousin marriage since his parents were related to each other as the children of first cousins.

The intellectual climate now is not averse to the view that personal histories may be relevant to academic interests. But shared aspects and differences between cousin marriages among Muslims, Jews or Christians, for whom such marriages are not taboo, for instance, is not sufficiently addressed apart from the overarching difference between personal and parental choice. But if parental or personal choice is taken as the overarching difference between cousin marriages, however, then perhaps one should be speaking of son-niece or daughter-nephew marriages, on the one hand, and cousin marriages on the other.

GENDER AND COUSIN MARRIAGE

Although Elementary Structures is a book set within a geographically and culturally delimited area, Lévi-Strauss's analysis of the place of women in kinship structures is thought provoking, to put it mildly. Lévi-Strauss puts forth the view that in simple societies, characterized by elementary structures of kinship, it is indeed the men who exchange women and not the other way around. Somewhat imperiously he declares that it makes no difference to his system if it is the women who exchange men, but empirically, as he puts it, in human societies it is the men who have exchanged women. Perhaps unwittingly, Lévi-Strauss gave a fillip to feminist scholarship.

The feminist questioning of a woman's place in a man's world developed by taking into account Lévi-Strauss' exposition of diverse societies. In one of the first reviews of *Elementary Structures*, Simone de Beauvoir read the page proofs, and wondered where these structures came from. She understood the book as a document that reflects 'the status of women in these societies' as well as her own. The search into the subjectivities of women had just begun with the publication of *The Second Sex*.

In another influential piece, Gayle Rubin (1974), too, asserts that the problem with women being the 'conduits' of a relationship, in Lévi-Straussian terms, is 'that they can't realize the benefits of their own circulation', as she puts it. What the book confronts us with, in her view, is a 'sex-gender system' elaborated in kinship terminologies and the social organization of marriage.

There is much in *Elementary Structures* for feminists and

masculinists to rue about. Although Lévi-Strauss does not use the word 'gender' in 'Elementary Structures', kinship and gender are, in fact, mutually constituted consistently throughout the book in my view. Through his compilation and analysis of kinship terminologies in diverse societies, Lévi-Strauss's work affords ample testimony to classifications by sex/gender that are ordered in Ego's own generation and those of ascendants and descendants. Within a sibling group, for instance, diverging matrimonial destinies are predicated on the basis of a sex/gender difference. In passing from Ego's own generation to the next, a change in the sex of the connecting relative, again, creates marriageable or unmarriageable cousins.

Biologically, cousins may indeed be equal but with Lévi-Strauss we are already in the world of socially constructed categories. He finds few 'feminist victories' in primitive societies but recognizes that bachelors can be the objects of mirth or ridicule as well. Lévi-Strauss notes that patrilineal and patrilocal regimes, such as those found in China, could be especially harsh on women. And perceptively cognizes the difference between unilineal clans and castes in that caste organization reckons with the status of both the mother and the father for its transmission. He sees women as constituting the bridges between nature and culture, not squarely in either camp, a nuanced analysis that resonates in the writing of later anthropologists such as Ortner.

Yet to ask how Lévi-Strauss's work is influenced by his being a man and based primarily on the work of male anthropologists is not irrelevant from a feminist perspective. I say this on two counts. First, re-worked ethnographies show that perspectives of women may have been eclipsed in earlier anthropological accounts. Women's perspectives and practices can, of course, be incorporated in the work of male and female anthropologists but women espoused the feminist perspective first, historically speaking. Such discourses, moreover, seldom show the 'unity of a logical architecture' to borrow Foucault's phrase, since women's strategies, more often than not, gnaw at the structure and modify it in minor ways without overturning it.

And how does the study of cousin marriage benefit by espousing a feminist perspective within anthropology?

Certain anthropological conventions come under the scanner. Cousin marriage that is described in anthropological conventions as patrilateral cross-cousin marriage and matrilateral cross-cousin marriage assumes the perspective of a male Ego. The difference between patrilateral and matrilateral cross-cousin marriage dissolves when a female Ego is brought into the picture. From this point of view, every matrilateral cross-cousin marriage is, simultaneously, for her husband a marriage with the patrilateral cross-cousin. Either way, it is based on B-Z connections. However, where it is the woman who shifts residence on marriage, marriage with the patrilateral cross-cousin emphasizes the patrifiliation of her marital destination. By contrast, marriage with her matrilateral cross-cousin, for a female ego, is contra Lévi-Strauss, not the Cheap Jack of marriage arrangements but a favoured practice that reinforces her mother's natal connections.

On the other hand, matrilateral parallel cousin marriage, by its relatively rare occurrence, attests to the weaker assertion of female-female links. The infrequent occurrence of marriages with the MZD, from a feminist perspective, arises from the cultural devaluation of Z-Z connections. On this front, there is no symmetry between matrilateral and patrilateral parallel cousin marriage since the former, by contrast with patrilateral cousin marriage, is seldom celebrated as pure or honourable. Yet, such marriages are valourized in the discourses of women, while in men's talk they are sometimes disguised as marriages with a classificatory patrilateral parallel cousin.

Further, Lévi-Strauss holds the view that a woman is always exchanged for another woman, almost as an axiom in the study of kinship systems. A sister may be exchanged for a spouse, in marriage by direct exchange, certainly. But where dowry or bride price play an overt role, this thesis seems stretched and non-kinship factors, too, enter the world of marital exchange. Again in regimes of matrilateral cross-cousin marriage and hypergamy, especially, women are seldom able to realize, as Gayle Rubin (1974) puts it, 'the value of their own circulation' for themselves.

Reviewing the history of marriages actually made, however, does bring out how women continue to inflect marriage choices. So that while agency does not rest overtly with the women, their views and interests are not entirely eclipsed. Although women may appear to be the objects to be exchanged at the point at which marriages are contracted, they do find ways of expressing their subjectivity over a lifetime. In this effort, however, religious, quasi-religious or local traditions that valorize patrilineal choices as the FBS/FBD marriage among Muslims, for instance, or the indirect exchange that privileges marriage with the matrilateral cross-cousin in south India, seldom ally with feminist interests.

Concluding Remarks

The marriage of cousins and the anthropological interest in the subject continues to be alive and kicking in India. Our understanding of such marriages undoubtedly profits from Lévi-Strauss's pioneering work on cross-cousin marriage. Anthropologists working in India still turn to him to make sense of the cousin marriage practices that they encounter, even as empirical enquiries refine the questions and go beyond the aspects that he explored. While dedicating *Structural Anthropology* to Emile Durkheim in the hundredth year of his birth, Lévi-Strauss declared that he is an 'inconstant disciple'. If we appear to be 'inconstant disciples' too, it is only because the mind-boggling diversity of cousin marriage practices looms larger than even Lévi-Strauss's remarkable study.

Lévi-Strauss's formidable theorizing blazed a trail, though from my vantage point today cross-cousins do not exhaust the universe of terms in the discourse on cousin marriage. But if cousin marriage and its study still persist it is perhaps because humans have not forgotten the elementary expressions of sociality which it affords and that Claude Lévi-Strauss illuminated for us so well.

Claude Lévi-Strauss, 2008
What Anniversary?

Vincent Debaene

When a chair of social anthropology was created at the Collège de France and awarded to Claude Lévi-Strauss, he started his opening lecture by mentioning a kind of personal myth attached to the number 8: the chair had been created in 1958; both Franz Boas and Durkheim, the two founders of social anthropology, were born in 1858; 300 years earlier, in 1558, the traveller Jean de Léry (whom Lévi-Strauss considered a forerunner of his own work) had encountered the Tupi Indians for the first time; Lévi-Strauss himself had met the Tupi 20 years earlier, in 1938, and so on. Lévi-Strauss did not mention, though it was implicit, that he was born in 1908, but his entry into the Bibliothèque de la Pléiade in 2008, the very year he turned 100 added another chapter to this little story and extended this myth to our present day.

This event created unexpected media frenzy. It graced the cover of *L'Express, le Point* and *le Nouvel Observateur* with headlines such as 'Le dernier des géants', 'le penseur du siècle', 'l'homme qui a révolutionné la pensée', and the like. Numerous special issues were (and still are) devoted to his work in magazines such as *le Magazine littéraire* or scholarly journals such as *Esprit*, the *Revue de philosophie*, and so on. Countless articles were devoted to the event in daily newspapers: *Le Monde, Le Figaro, Libération*, not to mention the radio and even TV shows.

A short word about La Pléiade: it is the most prestigious French literary series, from the publisher Gallimard. It was created in 1931 with the mandate to collect the masterpieces of French and world literature. The volumes are critical editions, full of annotations, comments, quotes from the manuscripts, edition variants, and so on. The very packaging of the books calls attention to their status as special, exemplary: they are provided in an elegant cardboard case, with the highest quality features, the pages are made of parchment paper and bound in leather with gold lettering on the spine; the compact size of the volumes makes them look like a small Bible.

Several elements about Lévi-Strauss's publication in the Pléiade attract attention: first of all, Lévi-Strauss entered the series during his lifetime, 'de son vivant'. This suggests an absolute consecration. It is not the first time that this has happened—that a living author has been welcomed into the Pléiade, but some things about this instance set it apart. First, Lévi-Strauss took an active part in this publication by virtue of the fact that he himself selected the works collected in the volume, and this is unprecedented. Many journalists have been quick to point out that the specialist of myth has himself become a living myth.

Furthermore, Lévi-Strauss is an anthropologist of the most scientific species. He is famous for having introduced an almost mathematical rigour into the study of human behaviour, particularly kinship. His work is renowned at once for the encyclopedic knowledge it displays, for its technical difficulty and for its abstraction. The fact that it is becoming part of the literary canon appears then all the more striking: not only is he a scientist, famous among his peers, but also a writer speaking to a larger audience.

Finally, part of the media frenzy likely stemmed from the fact that Lévi-Strauss himself remained unreachable throughout: he refused to give any interviews whether for newspapers or radio. So there was a kind of presence/absence game: he was very present because he was alive and he selected the works. But he was also out of reach, because he was incredibly old, and journalists only had archival footage to play on TV or radio, as if he were already dead. Some articles compared him to a lighthouse guard or to an old sentinel sending messages from very far away.

Such a reception might well be a topic for a cultural historian: one would identify in these events a very French attachment to literature, which is seen as part of national heritage and cultural identity. One might comment on a recent tendency toward commemoration and celebration; the nostalgia made possible by having a standpoint from which a (French) scholar could compare all cultures; the creation of the intellectual as a cultural hero, and so on. Although these questions are of the utmost interest, especially in an intercultural perspective, I would like to ask more directly: what was being celebrated? What was this anniversary? Was it the centenary of a birth? The 50 years since the publication of the seminal book, *Structural Anthropology*? The 40 years since the end of the so-called 'structuralist decade'?

Behind every anniversary lie the same questions: what was being commemorated and what does it mean *for us today*? This is also a very concrete, very simple question: why should I read Lévi-Strauss now? What will such a reading bring to me?

I will start with a very simple observation: an anniversary is not just one date; it is always the conflation of two dates. As such, it supposes temporality, the comparison between a before and a now, the assumption of a history and the production of a sense of history. The meaning of an anniversary is never a given; it is built through the confrontation between a past and a present; it can stress distance or proximity, progression or regression, permanence or discontinuity. So the question is: what is the underlying temporal model? What conception of history—or conceptions of history—are being silently mobilized?

I will first try to bring to light the temporal models which, to me, seem to lie behind the media celebration. How does the commemoration relate Claude Lévi-Strauss' work to time itself? I would like to explore the ways that this celebration is rooted in a specific conception of the divide between science and literature as a divide between two relationships to time. Then, I would like to try to use Lévi-Strauss's work, if not to contest the divide, then maybe to help us think of it in different terms—because, indeed, his work says a lot about the divide between science and literature.

★ ★ ★

If we ask 'what is Lévi-Strauss to us today?', the entry into the Pléiade the same year as his centenary is in itself an answer. As the work of Lévi-Strauss is solemnly consecrated as a national monument, this means that it will always be relevant to our times. It is integrated into the canon through a performative gesture: we make a bet on the future and at the same time prepare for such a future by decreeing: 'this work is immortal; it is part of those works to which it will always be good to go back.' This has been the classical scheme of the relationship between science and literature in France since the nineteenth century: a work which, *in its time*, was intended to be scientific later *turns into* literature and is decreed *timeless*.

The classical example of this type of elevation from science to literature is that of the naturalist Buffon. At the turn of the nineteenth century, his work was dismissed by the first generation of 'biologists', the ones who were embodying the shift from natural history to biology. Suddenly, Buffon's writings appeared out-of-date. I quote the naturalist Georges Cuvier who in many ways can be seen as Buffon's successor: Buffon was 'deluding himself with too many tropes'; he was depending too much on imagination and not enough on analysis and demonstration; he had 'procedural weaknesses that only the most trained scholars can be aware of'. However, said Cuvier, Buffon will nevertheless 'remain as one of our most eloquent and immortal writers'. This is a classical gesture: *what is lost for science may sometimes be rescued by style.* What has been passed over by the advancement of serious knowledge is abandoned but, in the same move, is restored in another dimension of time: the one of memory and oeuvres. Such a gesture is by no means specific to natural history; one could find numerous examples from historians or geographers. This is what happened to Michelet's work, for instance, at the end of the nineteenth century: academic historians came to the shared conclusion that his studies could not provide grounds for serious historical work, but they all also agreed that Michelet would remain unrivalled for his depictions of the French Revolution.

So in a way, that is what is happening with Lévi-Strauss' entry into the Pléiade. The media celebration is implicitly rooted in the Buffon model. It says: 'Never mind the diagrams; never mind the elementary structures of kinship; never mind the canonical formula of myth; forget the scientific ambition of an "inventory of mental patterns"'; Lévi-Strauss' work will remain *despite* his scientific ambition. What the anniversary means is precisely this: *the question of relevance has itself become irrelevant.* Lévi-Strauss' work is entering a new category, another region of our culture. The scientist might wonder 'what remains?' and might want to draw a line and distinguish between what is still relevant and what has become obsolete, but from a cultural standpoint, these questions don't matter anymore: the work will remain; something in it will always remain. The articles published on the eve of the centenary reveal that the criteria for Lévi-Strauss's consecration are similar to the ones which saved Buffon from oblivion: Lévi-Strauss will remain an 'immortal writer', a great stylist, a unique combination of 'esprit de finesse' and 'esprit de géométrie', and a perfect example of a very French tradition, which started with Montaigne, went through Montesquieu and Rousseau, and combines cultural relativism, curiosity for the exotic and meditation on human nature. He has joined the prestigious tribe of what Baudelaire called the 'phares'—the beacons.

Most of the time during the centenary excitement, there was another aspect as well: the consecration of the great anthropologist was seen as proof of the inherent insufficiency of anthropology and of the supreme position of literature in the hierarchy of discourses. According to many editorialists, by lionizing Lévi-Strauss as a writer, we are just reconnecting to a glorious past when literature and the study of man were undifferentiated. This was particularly obvious in the most conservative press. The entry into the Pléiade was seen as the rediscovery of a forgotten truth, which 50 years of kinship systems and structural analysis had overshadowed: that there is something in man which will always escape scientific discourse, a je-ne-sais-quoi that literature alone is able to grasp. I suppose that Lévi-Strauss' conservative positions on numerous issues fostered this interpretation, but it remains nonetheless true that conservative intellectuals were quick to see the entry into the Pléiade as an opportunity to revere Lévi-Strauss l'académicien (Lévi-Strauss is member of the most conservative literary institution in France: l'Académie française) while getting rid of Lévi-Strauss the structuralist. Paradoxically, this Pléiade was seen less as a recognition of the social sciences than as evidence of their insufficiency and their inability to reach their goal without the help of literature, style or poetry.

Such reasoning is not quite satisfying though, for at least two reasons. First of all, it is very unfaithful to Lévi-Strauss' thought. Lévi-Strauss has always described anthropology, if not as a science, at least as a discipline aiming at scientificness. He has always been very critical towards writers or literary scholars who, without training, method or empirical data, claim to have an 'anthropological' scope. He has even described the history of anthropology as a succession of revolutions similar to the revolutions in physics, comparing for example the theory of reciprocity to the theory of gravitation, the British anthropologist William Halse Rivers playing the role of Galileo, Marcel Mauss the role of Newton—and, I guess, although he did not mention it, himself being the Einstein of reciprocity. To Lévi-Strauss, if there should be a science of the human mind, it certainly won't occur *within* literature. So I am a little reluctant about a consecration which would celebrate Lévi-Strauss against himself.

Furthermore, such a reading of Lévi-Strauss' consecration relies on a great divide between science and literature and between their respective ability to increase our knowledge of humanity. I won't argue here that this divide is not legitimate. I won't try to show that writers and scientists are engaged in similar tasks and I won't try to unveil the rhetorical strategies used by scientists. To me, the question is not: 'is there a divide?' but how does the divide function? How is it used? I would now like to expand a little on that point because Lévi-Strauss' work actually provides very useful insights on that matter.

There are several ways to understand the difference between scientists and writers. One can contrast their methods and stage the difference as an opposition between explanation and interpretation. In this respect, literature is part of a general field devoted to understanding, as opposed to an explanation through causes and effects: the scientists are discovering laws where the writers are creating meaning. One can contrast their objects of study. This is a more romantic version of the divide: the principles of nature against the torments of the human heart; the fatality of the natural world against the unpredictability of human consciousness and action.

Finally, one can contrast their use of language—this is the most fashionable and common way to frame the opposition today: scientists use language as an instrument, in order to convey content and a clear message. For writers, language is not an instrument; it is the very substance of creation. It is Roland Barthes who framed the most sophisticated version of this distinction by opposing *écrivains* and *écrivants*, authors and writers. Scientists, says Barthes, have a non-problematic relationship with language whereas writers refuse to use language as a transparent medium; on the contrary, they play on its inherent opacity in order to raise questions about the way it shapes our world. The writer (*l'écrivant*) is teacher, scientist or anyone trying to transmit non-ambiguous information; even when he asks questions, his use of language is always assertive. As for the author (*l'écrivain*), he is renouncing any message; he uses the language as the sculptor uses the stone and this use is always interrogative, even when he asserts: 'The author radically absorbs the world's *why* in a *how to write*?'

As relevant as these distinctions may be to a certain extent, it may be worth remembering here a lesson of structural anthropology which considers not the content of an opposition but the way it functions and relates to other differences. It might be useful not to take the divide as natural and not to try to load it with positive content but to see how it relates to other differences. Indeed, when Cuvier dismisses Buffon as a scientist and promotes him as a writer, he is not distinguishing between two types of writings but between *two ways to relate them to time*: 'we *now* know that Buffon was deluding himself about the nature of organic molecules, but he will *remain* as one of our *immortal* writers.' In modern times, the identification of science, the very use of the adjective *scientific* is always indexed to a certain state of knowledge and to a progressive history. It is so pervasive that we don't even pay attention to it but any writing on a scientific matter or on science itself is always permeated with adverbs of time, always assuming a historical trend in which it locates itself: 'we now know...', 'we came to realize...', 'some still think that...'. And we can already note that the question 'what remains?' is, in its very form, assuming a progressive history which is typical of modernity.

There is another implication as well: if science is progressing, it means that the scientific content can be transmitted and passed down; in other words, the scientific text is translatable. Science and literature thus depend on two different temporal dimensions or two modes of time: on the one hand, the inescapable obsolescence of the scientific text; on the other hand, the permanence of the untranslatable work. Not only was Newton's work doomed to be surpassed from the very beginning, not only is a current graduate in physics more trained than Newton ever was, but Newton can be translated and summarized without any damage, which is not true of Homer, Balzac or Joyce. That is, I think, what Foucault had in mind when he was trying to shed light on the status of the scientific author: re-reading Newton today might lead us to reconsider the history of physics, but it will never change physics itself. The scientifically relevant content of Newton's text has been totally absorbed in the progress of physics. If we re-read Newton's work now, it cannot be for scientific motives.

In this respect, the distinction between *écrivains* and *écrivants* is not the most profound or the most fundamental. It is just a modern attempt to essentialize a cultural distinction. That being said, I don't mean that there is no difference between the scientist and the writer; there are indeed a lot, but what is most important is not an assortment of texts among which one could arbitrarily draw a line separating scientific from creative writings; what is most essential is the difference itself. To me, one of Lévi-Strauss' work's greatest contributions is to show not that this divide is arbitrary or random, but that, to be fully understood, it needs to be related to other oppositions.

In other words, I believe we can think through this entry into the Pléiade in a way that is not in tension with Lévi-Strauss's thinking but rather in a way that exploits it, and that we can use his work to rethink 'Buffon's model' (or the conversion of a text which *once* was scientific into a *timeless* monument) and to rethink the divide between science and literature.

Lévi-Strauss does not contest the divide but he allows us to think of it as a local version of some—if not universal, at least very widespread—patterns, by paralleling it with other divides in non-modern societies. I would like to stress two elements in Lévi-Strauss' work which are instructive in this respect.

The first one is his reflection on historical models. Lévi-Strauss is famous for having coined the distinction between what he calls 'cold' and 'hot' societies, basically non-modern or 'primitive' societies and cumulative modern societies. *Cold societies*, he argued, are like mechanical machines, such as clocks. They begin with a set amount of energy, and they continue to operate at the same level until some readjustment is necessary. *Hot societies* are like steam engines. They can do far more work than mechanical machines but they rapidly use up their energy and they must be constantly resupplied. Thus, 'hot' societies are constantly changing and have a clearly visible history, whereas cold societies resist change and attempt to continue operating in the same energy-conserving patterns as long as possible.

I won't have time here to enter the anthropological debate about this distinction. Contrary to what has often been said, Lévi-Strauss never stated that 'hot' societies were situated in history whereas 'cold' societies were situated outside of history; all societies are situated in history but what he calls 'cold' societies try to erase time and its effects altogether, especially through rituals and mythic recitations. Their customs, religious system and social organization stress stability and permanence rather than change and evolution.

And their entire ideology strives to negate the very possibility of something like a *historical event*. Let's just keep in mind that there are no pure 'cold' or 'hot' societies. All societies try to solve the inherent contradiction between permanence and irreversibility, between natural cycles and linear decay—or linear progress for that matter. But for the same reason, it would be a mistake to think of modern societies as entirely 'hot' or entirely cumulative. Instead, what is typical of modernity is not the assumption of a progressive history, but the special balance between a dominant historical trend dictated by the unquestionable progress of science and technology and the maintaining of some areas of permanence—namely artistic monuments. Even scientists like Cuvier, even the most radical advocates of progress always recognize that there are regions which escape from the diktat of constant renewal and from the erasing of the past by the present. In this respect, our divide between science and literature can be seen as the modern version of a line drawn by every society between permanence and linearity. From an anthropological perspective, art in modern societies is just the sanctuary of 'coldness' in predominantly 'hot' societies.

Another aspect of Lévi-Strauss' work might help us to re-qualify the divide between science and literature: his reflection on art. Modernity has defined art by the medium. The modern writer like the modern painter is no longer bound by the requirement of representation. Modernism claims to have freed itself from the constraints of pure depiction and seeks to focus instead on the exploration of the specific formal possibilities offered by each medium: language for the writer, colour and texture for the painter, and so on. But Lévi-Strauss shows that there is no such thing as a naïve art which would be captive to its concern for representation (either of natural or supernatural entities) and then, afterwards, a freer art which would liberate itself from such a concern and suddenly realize, through some leap of self-awareness, that the medium is not transparent. Through some decisive ethnographical analysis, Lévi-Strauss shows that the so-called 'primitive' or 'tribal' art does not ignore the opacity or the resistance of the medium, nor does classical figurative art. Every art form in every culture is engaging with the contingent and trying to make sense of contingency. This is the central thesis of the first chapter of *The Savage Mind* with its famous analysis of the small-scale model or miniature: every art is negotiating a balance between a reference, a medium and a function and the tendency of modernity to privilege the medium at the expense of the two others is just an option among others.

This, of course, merits further development and explanation but we can jump directly to the conclusion: 'Art lies half-way between scientific knowledge and mythical or magical thought' (*The Savage Mind*). It is a typically modern view to think of a two-fold divide between art and science. Lévi-Strauss encourages us to think rather in terms of a triadic distribution: art occupying an intermediary position between scientific thought and mythical thought.

Thus, there is a sort of permeability between art and science. Lévi-Strauss's most recent books—such as *The Story of the Lynx* or *Look, Listen, Read*—offer numerous and striking examples of passages from Delacroix's painting to fractal theory or from Rimbaud's poetry to recent discoveries in neurology. What matters is not that literature precedes or anticipates a science (which sooner or later will become obsolete) but the very possibility of a transition between the two orders. The two orders are separate, but it is possible to reconstruct and imagine intellectual transformations leading from one to the other. The work of art provides a sensitive synthesis of properties that science tries to isolate analytically. There is no rupture or conflict between science and art; the aesthetic experience is always an experience of knowledge. While science brings to light properties of matter or of the human mind, while mythical thought organizes the world with the data of sensory experience, art operates within the variety of the sensory world (such as mythical thought or 'bricolage') but, at the same time, constructs objects which, for the audience or the reader, are the occasion for both a sensory and intellectual experience. In a synthesis immediately given to perception, 'knowledge of the whole precedes knowledge of the parts'—to quote the famous phrase of *The Savage Mind*.

Thus, scientific thought is not a unique and autonomous intellectual activity, radically cut off from the other operations of the mind. There is no ontological rupture between art, myth and science. I quote from *Tristes tropiques*,:

> the work of the painter, the poet or the musician, like the myths and symbols of the savage, ought to be seen by us, if not as a superior form of knowledge, at least as the most fundamental and the only one really common to us all; scientific thought [being] merely the sharp point, more penetrating because it has been whetted on the stone of fact, but at the cost of some loss of substance.

I am well aware that these two aspects of Lévi-Strauss' work—his reflection on temporal models or on the relationship between art, scientific and mythical thoughts—merit further exploration. But at least the combination of these aspects provides grounds for rethinking the great divide between science and literature. Again, my purpose here is not to dismiss this divide as such, by saying, for example, that scientists (and especially social scientists) are writers like others and that, basically, all of them are engaged in the same task of writing persuasive fictions. Nor is it to reinforce the divide by saying that literature offers a specific and mysterious knowledge about man that social sciences will never grasp. It is just to think of this divide as relational to other divides—between progress and memory, between the translatable and the untranslatable, between the document and the monument, and so on. It is also a warning against any attempt to essentialize this divide either by reserving certain objects as literary and others as scientific or by defining science and literature by two different relationships to language. Science and literature might well define one another but neither the former nor the latter is an entity whose content or form can be predicted.

★ ★ ★

So to return to the original question, what does this anniversary and this entry into the Pléiade mean? Maybe simply the following: neither the blurring of the distinction between literature and social sciences, nor a consecration of literature *above* social sciences but, rather than a major turning point, a slight displacement, a subtle move which makes apparent some cultural divisions we take for granted, an opportunity to re-think the distribution of science and literature by paralleling it with other divides in non-modern societies.

As I said, this question about the meaning of the anniversary is also very simple, very concrete: why would I read Lévi-Strauss today? And this question is at once the most important and the hardest to answer. I would say that reading Lévi-Strauss is both an extremely demanding and an extremely rewarding experience. The richness of his work is precisely in this combination of rigour and pleasure and, to me, there is no reason to dismiss perishable knowledge so as to keep timeless style because if there is one lesson we should hold on to from his thought, it is that style and knowledge cannot be separated, and that our experience of art is always also an experience of knowledge.

In *Race and History*, Lévi-Strauss compares history to a card game with some sequences of accumulation and some moments of redistribution, some sequences of homogenization and some moves back to the diversity of the original hands that were dealt. If I can maintain the metaphor, then I would like to think of the 2008 anniversary not as a decisive shift, but maybe as a new hand being dealt and an invitation to play new games.

REFERENCES

Barthes, Roland. 1972 [1960]. 'Authors and writers', *Critical Essays*. Trans. Richard Howard. Evanston, Illinois: Northwestern University Press.

Charbonnier, Georges. 1969 [1961]. *Conversations with Claude Lévi-Straus*. Trans. John and Doreen Weightman. London: Cape.

Cuvier, Georges. 1861 [1826]. 'Éloge historique de Lacépède, lu le 5 juin 1826', *Recueil des éloges historiques lus dans les séances publiques de l'Institut de France*. Paris: Firmin-Didot.

Debaene, Vincent. 2010. *L'Adieu au voyage. L'ethnologie française entre science et littérature*, Bibliothèque des sciences humaines, Paris: Gallimard.

Foucault, Michel. 1984 [1969]. 'What Is an Author?', trans. Josue Harari, in *The Foucault Reader*, ed., Paul Rabinow. New York: Pantheon Books.

Kaplan, Alice and Roussin, Philippe. 1996. 'A changing idea of literature: the Bibliothèque de la Pléiade', *Yale French Studies*, no. 89.

Lévi-Strauss, Claude. 1963 [1956]. 'Do Dual Organizations Exist?', *Structural Anthropology*, vol. 1, trans. Claire Jacobson and Brooke Grundfest Schoepf. New York: Basic Books.

———. 1966 [1962]. *The Savage Mind*. Chicago: University of Chicago Press.

———. 1973 [1955]. *Tristes tropiques*, trans. John and Doreen Weightman. London: Cape.

———. 1976 [1952]. 'Race and History', in *Structural Anthropology*, vol. 2. Trans. Monique Layton. New York: Basic Books.

———. 1976 [1960]. 'The Scope of Anthropology', in *Structural Anthropology*, vol. 2. Trans. Monique Layton. New York: Basic Books.

———. 1995 [1991]. *Story of Lynx*, trans. Catherine Tihanyi. Chicago: The University of Chicago Press.

———. 1997 [1993]. *Look, Listen, Read*, trans. Brian C.J. Singer. New York: Basic Books.

Mythologique
The Structural Method of Claude Lévi-Strauss

Harjeet Singh Gill

The study of myths, as demonstrated by Lévi-Strauss, leads us to an understanding of the mental complexities of the human mind, of the intellectual incisions of both individual and collective order, and, of the correlations and confrontations of man with his environment. In its form, a myth is 'surrealistic', in content, it represents the materialist history of a people.

A myth is always a product of an individual in the beginning, but as soon as it is created, it undergoes a series of transformations due to further individual or collective reflections, or attempts at cultural mediations. Through this continuous process of generation of one structure into another, certain sections of the basic structure remain the same, others of the 'probabilist' level are constantly altered through oral transmission. All individual works are potential myths, but it is their adoption by the people as a collective heritage, and, the realization of the transformations on their probabilist contours that bestows on them the status and the dignity of myths. Since the myths of a culture are a product of incessant dialectical transformations, they represent extremely complex wholes of structures within a Structure. A myth is a combination of numerous residues of the past. In its diamond like crystallization, it is a challenge to the human intellect to decipher its contours which have undergone changes over the centuries, and are presented to us in their utmost precision. A myth is thus a mosaic of extremely fine pieces juxtaposed in correlations which defy all attempts of descriptive statements.

The structures of the various versions of a myth explain each other. The dialectical process in the creation of myths leads us from one myth to another. As such, the myths 'talk' to each other. They communicate with each other in terms of their combinatory systems which have necessary correspondences. Since in their different versions we observe the evolution of one structure into another, the study of myths sheds light on the very nature of human mental structures which are responsible for all these mediations. Myths are the most dense depositories of cultural symbols, a proper comprehension of their significance requires a detailed analysis of their various aspects, which, as has been well demonstrated by Lévi-Strauss, cover such vast domains as botany, astronomy, zoology, ethnography, linguistics and anthropology. A thorough understanding of these branches of knowledge is imperative to comprehend what Lévi-Strauss calls the infrastructure of the myths.

It is with this infrastructure that the successive transformations of a myth are related. All modifications are operated upon outer contours. The inner core or the nuclear structure remains the same, the rest of the structure is in a perpetual state of disequilibrium. The understanding of the structuration of myths requires an insight into the nature of diachronic alterations. All transformations are conscious mediations and conscious reflections on the contradictions of life. To reflect upon these mediations, a social scientist follows the path of 'knowledge', of becoming conscious of the material-object of his study. The role of the individual is that of the 'thinking', 'conscious' individual. It is the thinking, reasoning individual who reflects upon the Other object, the object-myth, the object-culture, the material object. As such, as Lévi-Strauss argues, the role of the reasoning individual before the myths is the same as that of the physical scientist before his material objects. Mythologiques, thus strictly speaking, is a conceptualization of the things of the world, is of the order of intellect, of logic. There is no place for the ambiguities introduced due to a vague subject under the camouflage of human 'liberty'. The liberty of man is his intellectual faculty which can mediate and transform one material structure into another.

If this is the object of study, it is obvious that the method that is employed to analyse it cannot possibly be called descriptive or synchronic. It is certainly a diachronic reconstruction, most of the material it works on is oral, not recorded in the usual sense of the term. This reconstruction is structural like André Martinet's linguistic reconstructions in his *Economie des changements phonétiques* (1955). It does not deal with individual, disparate elements. It is not simply a question of analysing the frozen, synchronic structures of the so-called 'cold societies'. These cold societies at a given time evolved from a dynamic hot past and their structures evolved through numerous structural transformations. There is always a proto myth that undergoes structural changes in the prehistoric past. The various versions of the same myth demonstrate the complex interactions leading to further transformations and mutations. This method of Lévi-Strauss follows the outlines of the diachronic phonology of André Martinet and not the synchronic phonology of the Prague School advocated by Roman Jacobson as is generally assumed. It may be underscored here that Lévi-Strauss, Jacobson and Martinet were all together in New York after the Second World War.

In his *Mythologiques*, Lévi-Strauss began from the southern hemisphere and progressively moved on to the northern. The infinite variations in the myths were taken as both a point of departure and as a co-reference. An extensive sum of information on geography, geology, magic, religion and art was utilized to decipher the various details. The texts of the myths were studied with as much care as it was possible, considering the differences in linguistic grouping and textual components. Lévi-Strauss, however, explains that the exact linguistic information was quite useful but not absolutely indispensable as the myths represent significant conceptual structures where the process of transformation on specific aspects of structures fill all possible gaps. The myths are like surrealistic images whose epithets are of an order different from that of ordinary language.

The transformational process of myths is interminable. A myth is an open system. It is incessantly and constantly in evolution, for the simple reason that human intellect never stops to function. As such, the mythical discourse follows the control of the Saussurian concept of langue. The mythical transformations are of the order of parole. During the process of transformations there are erosions and fragmentary drop-outs which condense mythemes into highly complex images. A myth is apprehended only in its 'becoming', in its process of transmission where the probabilist aspects need to be isolated for a proper comprehension of the mythematic structures. The interrelationships of the different elements present different types of symmetries and a hierarchy of contradictions and their inversions. Such contradictions can be analysed following the theory of categories, as systems based on both the ensemble of terms and the ensemble of relations between these terms, argues Lévi-Strauss. It corresponds well with the notion of 'morphism'. These tools of epistemology can be fruitfully used in the analysis of the myths provided the material nature of the text-object is not obliterated.

Lévi-Strauss deals with the objections of the existentialist philosophy at length, which attempts to introduce individual 'subjectivity' in the name of finding a proper place for man in the scheme of things. The scientific investigation of man and his environment cannot, however, be conducted at a subjective level. The Cartesian cogito is a thinking cogito. The relationship of man with his universe is purely intellective. The study of the structures of myths aims at understanding the semiological functioning of man's relation with his material products. In the overall perspective of the mythologique, the science of the study of myths, what is at stake is not the abstract questions of the destiny of man or the problematics of the origin of mankind, which is generally the manifest structure of many a myth, but the ethnographic, cultural, religious and the material world, which is a 'real' world. All mythical reflections have a sound basis in human nature, which is again, an empirical reality.

The problem with existentialist philosophy, centred on the imaginary subject, believes Lévi-Strauss, is its ethnocentricism. The 'effects' of the means of material production and their relationships are different in different geographical and cultural regions. The existentialist philosophy attempts to explain all humanity in terms of the conclusions drawn from an analytical study of a given cultural complex beginning with the Hellenic tradition. The problematics does not centre around the place of man in this world, but of which man. Each culture defines its man by its own infrastructure and superstructure. Everywhere, it is man whose consciousness leads to historical and cultural mediation. The myths represent the history of each ethnic man for the last thousands of years. The mythical transformations are due to intellectual interventions, and, the study of the myths is squarely placed in the context of these hierarchies of structural modulations, which gives us information on man, not expected by existentialist philosophy.

The myths as vehicles of cultural mediations are concrete objects while existentialist philosophy tends to deal with abstract objects, says Lévi-Strauss. In a myth, we attempt to hear the great anonymous voice of its people, submerged in its profound depths. The existentialist philosopher is face to face with himself, instead of confronting the real world around him. He leaves aside the universe of variations of history and ethnology on which are based the so-called savage societies.

After philosophy, Lévi-Strauss follows his argument with reference to literature, art and music. In this context, a very interesting phenomenon has been the underlying patterns of systems which have undergone successive transformations, and, as such, are structurally very significant. Not every object can be submitted to that kind of analysis, nor can the structures be artificially created. Structures are natural phenomena which have a diachronic evolution, and whose disequilibrium is a resultant of a long-drawn-out process. Ignoring this fundamental characteristic of cultural structures, there have been, in recent times, some naive attempts at constructing artificial structures in literature, art, and even in music. These structures are, in no way, of the same qualitative order, which have been discovered and perpetuated over several centuries. They lack the fundamental inter-structural relationships. For example, the question of regional structures within a global structure cannot even be posited in this context. Structural analysis deals with already constituted structures, which have by definition, seen the ravages of history. The structures of myths and language belong to that category. They are natural structures with an inbuilt characteristic of human praxis. They are as such different from the structures of physical sciences. The physical sciences deal with the symbols of things as such, but the human sciences deal with the symbols of things which have already attained the status of symbols.

Lévi-Strauss believes that the so-called original text of a myth does not exist. By the time a narrative attains the status of a myth, it is already a 'translation' or an interpretative mediation of the original event. Either its earlier version is found in the adjoining culture, or in another myth, whose transformation it represents. What an analyst deals with is necessarily a 'deformed' version. However, the study of myths is concerned primarily with these deformations, for each of these transformations is a result of a dialectical juxtaposition of another transformation, and, their essence lies in the irreducible fact of this translation 'by' and 'for' this opposition. From this point of view, a myth is not situated in a given language or a given culture, but from the point of view of its articulation, in another language, and in another culture. A myth, as such, is never of the language, it is a perspective of another language. Lévi-Strauss believes that the substance of a myth is neither in its style, nor in the manner of its narration, nor in its syntax, but in its 'history'.

This is why the comparison of myth with music is most relevant. A myth is translatable into another melody, which preserves a rapport of homology with it. It can be transcribed in different tones. It can be converted from major to minor, and, vice-versa. It can act on the parameters which transform its rhythm, its resonance, and, its emotive charge. In music, it is always a question of 'conversions' or transformations on the same theme. All the same, if it is possible to translate one melody into another, one kind of music into another, one can never, as in the case of myths, translate music into something other than itself.

There is a striking parallel between mythical recitation and musical composition, argues Lévi-Strauss. He says that there are four types of objects for the study of structures, the mathematical 'being', natural languages, musical works, and myths. The mathematical entities consist of structures of absolutely pure state. They entertain a rapport of correlation and opposition with the elements of languages, or following Saussure, they have two aspects of sound and significance, which are the products of their very interaction. In music, the structure, in a way, adheres to sound, and not to its significance. In mythology, it is just the opposite. The mythical structure derives its being from its significance.

The mathematical entities are independent of both sound and significance, both expression and content. A natural language represents a union of these two aspects. The musical structures depend more on sound, and, the mythical structures are based primarily on their patterns of significance. Music and myths are thus sub-products of a translation of a given earlier structure, operated upon language. There can be no music without an underlying language. Music is a language without significance, a pure form of language. The significance of the form of music is provided by the audience. The transformations in myths carry parameters of semantic structures without necessarily carrying with them the precise linguistic articulations.

More than their rapport with language, the correspondence between music and myth is in the manner of their composition. The recitation of music depends upon alliterations and repetitions, upon the linear sequence, as well as the re-introduction of the same elements after certain intervals. The narration of a myth is supported by language, by intonation, and by several other gestures. In music, the significance is completely outside its sound, and hence depends largely on the 'effect' it has on the auditor.

The successive transformations of the myths present their structures as boxes within boxes as a series of interconnected structures. These modulations are due to the semiological control of the dialectics of semantic categories which reorganize the ensembles of significance. In music, the two principal means of composition are (a) the confrontation of one structure with another, and, (b) their maintenance by transforming their significant support, or what is called, their development. The musical language detaches itself progressively from its distinctive character in a way that the latest structures are always employed as a means of their support. It is across the variations of sub-structures that the traditional music maintains its individual character. A structure is accessible by means of its homomorphism. A work of music is a system of sounds which is capable of introducing significance in the spirit of the auditor.

One can say that the musical communication and the linguistic communication presuppose the union of sound and significance, but the nature of relationship in both of these cases is not the same. Within a society, there is no dialogue about the myth, all discussion is excluded. The dialectics of comprehension is carried on through transformations. The same is true of music. These transformations develop images, symbols or intense structures, as in music, which overwhelm their audience by their density. They envelop the spirit of the one who participates in these images or melodies. Their very forms or their expressive articulations are their significance. In each case, it is an affair of cultural participation. Since it is primarily an affair of one structure leading to another, there can be no comprehension of either music or myth without a previous conscious contact with the earlier structures. Different transformations must be correlated for their proper understanding.

In its condensed form, a myth appears at two distinct modalities. At times, it is explicit as in its narration, and is explained in terms of its internal organizations. At others, a myth is manifested in the form of fragmentary notes, in its implicit form, such as in a ritual. A myth is a combination of both the narrative as such and the ritual. Some social scientists separate the two and study them as different entities. However, one explains the other. The existence of the mode of mythology leads us to believe that in it implicitly, it resembles most the sacred music, the symbol and the image. The structure of the mythical narration is not only interrelated with that of ritual but most often depends on it. This ritualistic aspect of the myth is non-verbal. Its articulation is of a different order. It is integrated in the psyche and the intellect of a culture in a way different from the simple narrative which is a sort of a support that helps decipher the 'frozen' images. The ritual is like the pure music which exists outside language. The structure of the ritual is studied like the structure of the instrumental music which gets occasional support from vocal music for its continuation, so is the role of the narrative in a myth.

This elaboration is produced at two levels: by the progressive decomposition of the syntagm, and by the crisscrossing of the paradigm. The one corresponds to an axis which can be called 'metonymic'. It substitutes for each totality, the parts that it separates, and treats each of these in turn as relative totalities of a subordinate order, where is exercised the same work of decomposition. Thus, behind each pair of primary oppositions, emerge secondary oppositions, and, behind them, tertiary, and so on, until the entire oppositional operation is complete.

The other axis, which is properly speaking that of the myth, is 'metaphoric'. It subsumes the individualities under a paradigm. It extends or contracts the concrete given facts, helping them cross the fragmentary discontinuities, which separate the empirical order from the symbolic order, and finally, from the imaginary and the schematic order. The constant reference in the ritual to non-verbal expressions, to gestures and symbols, renders the task of understanding quite difficult, for the ritualistic thought progresses on the perpendicular axes, and as such, the distance between their 'origin' and the actual realization is extended with each new structuration.

It needs to be emphasized here that all forms of natural art correspond to this aspect of mythical structuration. It is always a structural complexity of the simple narrative, or the parts which are easily accessible to the synchronic reference with proper syntactic organization and symbolic images which are impregnated in the cultural memory at a subconscious level. In this context, there is also the question of the archetypal images of a given culture, and, the images which have a rather fluid nature, or are in the process of acquiring the status of cultural significations across various diachronic evolutions. The history of the transformations of the ritualistic, symbolic aspect of the myth as such is much more complicated, and as Lévi-Strauss has rightly pointed out, in structural analysis we deal not only with 'primary' oppositions, and 'secondary' oppositions, but behind each pair, there is a set of 'tertiary' oppositions, and so on. The structural analysis is a continuous process.

The investigation of myths is an open-ended investigation. There is the overall global structure of the langue of the myth that ensures its consistency and continuity, but the incessant transformations due to the dialectics at the level of parole lead an investigator in all possible directions. As Lévi-Strauss has demonstrated with brilliant detours, each reference to an animal, plant, planet, custom, mask, human behaviour, leads the mythologist in search of all possible physical, concrete and enthnographic information which is essential for establishing proper correlations amongst different elements of the myth. Also, since parts of the myth appear only in fragmentary notes, their cohesive relations of the past having been frozen, this vast ethnographic information of botany, zoology, astronomy, and religious practices helps fill the gaps. The comprehension of myths requires the skill of diachronic reconstructions of the highest order, for it is not a question of assembling together all sorts of information, but it is an affair of putting together all the jigsaw pieces in their proper setting. As such, mythologique is historiography par excellence. It aims at reintegrating man in his nature, the man who is lost, in terms of Rousseau, in the disorganized inequality of our culture and society.

Finally, in the Indian context, I would like to refer to a very incisive analysis of the evolution of the Janam Sakhis around the life of Guru Nanak (1469–1538). There are mainly four texts which record the various myths and legends associated with the life of the founder of Sikhism. All of them were written at least a hundred years after the Guru's demise. During this long period, the narratives were preserved, evolved and interpreted in the oral tradition. In these four texts there are narratives which are short anecdotes, others more elaborate, still others with several interpolations. In each case, there is an overall discourse that determines the delineative and the interpretative function of a specific anecdote. W. H. McLeod in his *Early Sikh Tradition*(1980) has presented an extremely analytical and incisive interpretation of every step of the development and integration of each discursive formation. With a brilliant postmodern dialectical incision he has demonstrated how a given legend evolved from a proto anecdote, and how in the successive stages of its development, it was administered a number of interpolations and interventions.

In the universe of the *Mythologiques* there is a constant reference to birds, animals, stars. The animate and inanimate worlds merge in a newly constituted universe where human and non-human lose all their preconceived distinctions. In the universe of the Janam Sakhis, McLeod analyses the dialectics of anthropology and cosmology that constitutes a metaphysical universe that never loses contact with historical interpolations. In this historiography of the discourse of Guru Nanak, McLeod delineates the contours of the evolution of the narratives with incessant conceptual interactions in the domain of the world within and the world without. Within the universe of this discourse, in the domain of the imaginaire and the empirical, the sacred and the profane, we witness historical and theological creativity of the highest order. I do not know whether McLeod was inspired by the researches of Lévi-Strauss but it is certain that in the reconstructive, diachronic methodology, there is a striking resemblance. In any case, by the 1970s, the French structuralist movement had crossed the channel and the intellectual universe all over had undergone a decisive transformation. The predominant structural framework had replaced the simple chronological or even synchronic, metonymic descriptions. All discursive formations were being studied with a constant back and forth in the syntagmatic and the paradigmatic or the metonymic and the metaphoric order. The emphasis was on the study of the *becoming of the structures* which were always uneven, with more or less functional load in one or other aspect of its combinatory system. Lévi-Straussian structuralism never believed in readymade structures.

REFERENCES

Haudricourt, A. 'Richesse en phonemes et richesse en locuteures', L'Homme, 1961.

Hjelmslev, L. 'Prolegomena to a theory of language', trans. F.J. Whitfeld. Baltimore, 1953.

Jakobson, R. 'Preliminaries to speech analysis', Cambridge, Mass., 1952.

Lévi-Strauss, Claude. 'La pensee sauvage', Plon, 1962.

———. 'Le cru et le cuit', Plon, 1964.

———. 'Du miele aux cendres', Plon, 1967.

———. 'L'origine des manieres de table', Plon, 1968.

———. 'L'Homme nu', Plon, 1971.

Martinet, A. 'Economie des changements phonétiques', Berne, 1955.

McLeod, W. H. 'Guru Nanak and the Sikh religion', Oxford, 1968.

Lévi-Strauss or Sartre?
Kant and the Savage Mind

PRADEEP A. DHILLON

'It remains possible that the theory of perception, ideally starting from a blind intuition, may end compensatorily with some empty concept, and that judgement, the counterpart of pure sensation, may degenerate into a general function of an indifferent linking of objects, or even become once more a psychic force detectable in its effects.'[1]

In the preface to *The Savage Mind,* Claude Lévi-Strauss refers to the debates and disagreements that existed between him and Jean-Paul Sartre regarding the philosophical foundations of anthropology. It is worthwhile revisiting the key aspects of their disagreement for many of the issues in contemporary social science research, in the wake of the linguistic—or postmodern—turn in anthropology, are reminiscent of these earlier debates.[2]

French post-structuralist theorists, critically aware of the oppressive structures of knowledge that a binary approach to understanding the world provides us, left in their wake the ruins of systematic philosophy with its broader epistemic claims that sought to go beyond the

---

[1] Merleau-Ponty, *Phenomenology of Perception* ([1945] 2002), Routledge:New York p. 37.

[2] See, for example, the World Social Science Report', http://www.universityworldnews.com/article.php?story=20100828050924443.

particular knowledge. In other words, narrative and ethnographic accounts of the particularity of experiences and events became the privileged modes of representing knowledge and rendering suspect any attempt at providing a systematic understanding of the phenomena in question. Perhaps no term, within the academic sophistications of the last 25 years, was pronounced more defunct than systematic philosophy—the antagonism afforded it superseded only by that effected by the term 'reason'. We, as emerging intellectuals in the 1980s, were enjoined to struggle towards epistemological freedom, by carefully dismantling texts in order to lay bare patriarchal, colonial, and all other systems of domination that lay buried in the presuppositional structures of academic discourse. Philosophy was the scalpel that would lay bare these hidden agendas of hegemony even as it was turned on itself to dismantle its own regimes of totalization, and oppressive rationalism. The positive task, if one dared venture beyond such passionate deconstruction was to describe, describe, describe—and historicize, historicize, historicize. That is, the demands that post-structural thinking placed on scholarship was to turn us all into ethnographers. In so doing, the debate between Jean-Paul Sartre and Claude Lévi-Strauss came to be written large within academic discourse. I want to demonstrate that Jacques Derrida, for example, would have been a more suitable target for the sorts of charges Sartre brought against Lévi-Strauss, even as Lévi-Strauss himself provides a corrective to both Sartre and Derrida. In my brief remarks here, I suggest that we would do well to pay attention to the philosophical underpinnings of Claude Lévi-Strauss's arguments if we are not to fall into the abyss of exponentially multiplying accounts of ever smaller, mutually exclusive, domains of activity and experience. In so doing, I suggest, we run the risk of dividing our worlds into ever smaller, epistemologically impenetrable fragments, at the very moment our histories demand border-crossing conversations, and mutual regard.

What, then, is the nature of the dissension between Sartre and Lévi-Strauss? In Strauss's own words: 'The problem is to what extent thought that can and will be both anecdotal and geometrical may yet be called dialectical.'[3] Through an exquisite use of irony, Lévi-Strauss conflates the 'savage' mind with the human mind. Through the use of a range of examples from the most particular of artefacts to abstract representations, he demonstrates that there is nothing that remains alien to the so-called 'savage' mind, and the principle of dialectical reason can be found in the mind reaching out to make sense of the world that the 'savage', hence all humans, inhabit. In other words, while exploring narratives of difference, Lévi-Strauss provides insight into how the **human** mind works. He studies particularities, and carefully makes a quasi-universal epistemic claim.

Lévi-Strauss's disagreements with Sartre turn on two important points: first, as an anthropologist, one whose labour is typically tied up with descriptions of the particular, he stands accused by Sartre, of focusing on the aesthetic-perceptual dimension of knowledge rather than providing understanding. Second, he differs from Sartre on the meaning and use of the term 'dialectical reason'. I believe that we can get a clearer picture of what is at stake in this debate for Lévi-Strauss when we remember that he was trained in philosophy under the tutelage of a Kantian, and was a friend of Maurice Merleau-Ponty—the philosopher of perception, knowledge, and the mind.[4]

Let us take the first objection—that Lévi-Strauss' deep interest in the particularity of experiences in different cultures renders

---

[3] Claude Lévi-Strauss, *The Savage Mind*.

[4] It is interesting to note that the Kant scholar at the University of Illinois, sometimes refers to Merleau-Ponty as 'Kant with legs'. Merleau-Ponty follows Kant in thinking about the interplay between structures of the mind and experience in the making of knowledge, but with the additional recognition of the importance of thinking about the knowing subject as embodied.

him an 'aesthete' since he, according to Sartre, studies humans as if they were ants. What Sartre objects to first, is the epistemological premise, namely the interplay between perception and experience in the making of knowledge; and second, to the attention that anthropology pays to the particular details of the cultural webs of belief and practice within which individual and societal lives are lived out—but at one level of abstraction. That is, Sartre also objects to the efforts made by Lévi-Strauss to move away from empirical details to provide a more general sense of the differences and similarities that lie among and between various human organizations. Lévi-Strauss rightly argues that Sartre, at the very least, contradicts himself when he thinks of culture as a condition to be overcome, or as a site of resistance to the reduction of social practices to systems of representations. In other words, for Sartre, culture either asks that we break free from it, or refuse the reduction of the richness of our lived experiences to patterns of human thought and action that we might potentially share with others in different times and places. Thus, Sartre, as Lévi-Strauss rightly notes, is at risk of placing the 'savage', or the 'victim', in opposition to those who are not primitive, are civilized, and have to a large extent realized their freedom of will through resisting their specific historical and cultural conditions. In so doing, for Lévi-Strauss, Sartre reproduces the very conditions and structures of oppression that he is purportedly trying to repudiate. The Indian art historian, Partha Chatterjee, is worth quoting when thinking about the production of knowledge within the complex of global hierarchies, and power:

> The French philosopher, Jean-Paul Sartre, once stated that Surrealism was stolen from the Europeans by 'a Black [the poet Aimee Cesaire]' who used it brilliantly as a tool of Universal Revolution. Sartre's admiring but enigmatic comment encapsulates the problematic relationship between non-Western

artists and the international avant-garde, which is enmeshed in a complex discourse of authority, hierarchy, and power.[5]

Through his insistence on the particular, Sartre, the philosopher, jeopardizes his entire project of dissolving the distinction between person and person, and humans and nature. What Lévi-Strauss, the resolute anthropologist, offers instead, through a simultaneous assemblage of the particular events and experiences and broader patterns of culture, is a reminder that each of the hundreds and thousands of societies which have existed side by side in the world or succeeded one another since man's first appearance, has claimed that it contains the essence of all the meaning and dignity of which human society is capable, its claim has in its own eyes rested on a moral certainty comparable to that which we can invoke in our own case.[6]

Thus, the Mayans' claim of moral certainty for The Popul Vuha is no less robust than that offered by the Bhagvad Gita or the Bible.[7] In other words, Sartre's emphasis on particularity encourages the rewriting of modes of thinking within the oppositional framework of 'primitive' and 'civilized' and making related claims of moral development and knowledge that close examination of the systems of beliefs in different societies would not support. Furthermore, Lévi-Strauss points out, that such claims which arise out of a lack of knowledge of, and familiarity with, systems of thought that are not our own, often lead to the belief that humans reside, alongside each other, in mutually exclusive historical and geographical units of being, when in truth we reside in a system of differences and

---

[5] Partha Chatterjee, *The Triumph of Modernism: India's Artists and the Avant-Garde, 1922-1947,* London: Reaktion Books, p. 7.

[6] Lévi-Strauss, *The Savage Mind.*

[7] See, Pradeep A. Dhillon, 'Unhomely Readings of Philosophy's Fictions', *Thesis Eleven,* 44, 1996, pp. 87–99.

similarities. In locking oneself into the particularities of our own thinking we lose sight of knowledge of humans in general and become imprisoned by our Cartesian cogitos. For Lévi-Strauss, there is little difference between how Sartre thinks about his environment and the manner in which a Melanesian does. This is not a mere moral platitude on Lévi-Strauss's part. Rather, just as he is able to demonstrate the limits placed on Sartre's thoughts by his Cartesian commitments, so too we could argue that Lévi-Strauss's claims are based on a rigorous Kantian epistemology.

In his introduction to the idea of a transcendental knowledge, Kant argues that for all of us, Frenchmen and Melanesian women alike, knowledge springs from two sources: first, the power of receiving impressions through the faculties of our mind, and second our ability to form and cognize these representations. Through the first an object is given to us, and through the second, it is placed in relation to this first to constitute what we might call an episteme—a knowledge 'object'. Intuitions, the impressions that we receive, and conceptions, constitute the elements that are the cause of all our knowledge. These elements are placed in a relation such that conceptions without intuition, or intuitions without conception cannot afford us cognition. Or, famously, in Kantian terms, concepts without intuition are empty, and intuitions without concepts are blind.[8] Cartesians who seek to arrive at truths through introspection alone run the grave risk of arriving at conclusions that are either trivially true, limited in scope of application, or outright wrong. Both thought and experience are vital to the making of responsible knowledge claims. Empirical engagement is necessary in order to arrive at judgements that might suitably qualify as truth. It is in this

---

[8] 'Empty Thoughts and Blind Concepts', in response to Leonard Waks, 'Intuition in Thinking: Teaching and Learning without Thinking,' *Philosophy of Education*, University of Illinois Press, 2006, pp. 389–91.

sense that Lévi-Strauss claims that, 'anthropology is the principle for all research, while for Sartre it raises a constraint to be overcome or a resistance to reduce.'[9] In other words, Lévi-Strauss endows anthropology with an epistemic-philosophical status whereas Sartre uses it as a descriptive term for the conditions within which we find ourselves, and want to free ourselves from.

Furthermore, following Kant, we could argue that the substance of our minds is such that receiving impressions through our faculty of intuition can never be other than sensuous. On the other hand, the ability to spontaneously produce representations, we call understanding. But it is important to reiterate that neither takes precedence over the other. Without the sensuous faculty no object would be given to us, and without the faculty of understanding no object would be thought. Thoughts without content are void. Intuitions without conceptions are blind. Neither can be exchanged for the other. Knowledge arises from the united operation of both. Nevertheless, the difference between these two epistemological poles cannot be overlooked.[10] We need to make a clear distinction between sensibility, which is the aesthetic dimension of knowing, and understanding that is derived through logic. In other words, when Sartre accuses Lévi-Strauss of studying humans like ants and of being an aesthete, he is accusing him of either reducing the epistemological moment to logic and understanding—through his efforts at systematization of the differences and similarities to be found in the hundreds of thousands of societies that exist in the world—or to a focus on the local and the particular as his ethnographic labours would reflect. What Sartre misses in Lévi-Strauss's philosophically informed methodology is the constitutive

---

[9] Lévi-Strauss, *The Savage Mind*, p. 249.

[10] For telling examples of this, see the introduction to Maurice Merleau-Ponty's *The Phenomenology of Perception*, Routledge, [1945] 2002.

nature of thought and experience in epistemological constructivism that is a feature of all human knowledge—Frenchman and Melanesian women alike.

Ironically, as argued earlier, Sartre himself runs aground in his refusal of anthropological experience and his epistemological commitments to Cartesian introspection. When Lévi-Strauss points out that Sartre's methodological concerns for putting oneself in the historical other's shoes is a practical rather than theoretical point, he is pointing to the limits of Sartrean thick description. Such a description, or phenomenology, as he rightly points out, is a place of departure for anthropology, not its arrival. A good ethnography helps us develop sophisticated knowledge about what truly divides us, and what lines of resonance are possible. Within our contemporary context it is perhaps trivial to point out that this debate is still with us—what is not so trivial is the renewed interest in the significance of Kantian epistemology after post-structural engagements with ethnographic narratives.

Jacques Derrida, too, in his criticism of Lévi-Strauss as a rationalizer of difference has missed the aesthetic pole of Lévi-Strauss' method.[11] This is the pole that Sartre, in his misreading of Lévi-Strauss, criticizes him for embracing too tightly, and hence levels the accusation of 'aesthete' at him. One might have expected in Derrida's reading of Lévi-Strauss in the second part of his 'Structure, Sign and Play' a recognition of a common ground or intention. For Lévi-Straussian anthropology, at every point, is an implied criticism of western logic, and its rationalism, scientism, and ethnocentrism. But instead, as the philosopher Lena Petrovic so ably points out, Derrida accuses Lévi-Strauss of perpetuating precisely the rationalist, ethnocentric logic that was Lévi-Strauss'

---

[11] Jacques Derrida, *Of Grammatology*, tr. by Gayatri C. Spivak, Johns Hopkins University Press, [1976] 1998.

intention to criticize.[12] Derrida claims that Lévi-Strauss bases his whole argument on the opposition between nature/culture, but it is important to note that Lévi-Strauss repeatedly insists that this distinction is untenable. Universality, he argues, is no doubt the attribute defining natural phenomena, yet incest, which is a set of cultural prohibitions, is also found to be universal. Lévi-Strauss calls this self-erasure of the difference that hitherto seemed a self-evident truth a scandal. Yet although he admits that the opposition culture/nature can no longer be relied on as having any truth value, he nevertheless pursues his analysis in the hope that terms like 'nature' and 'culture' are, if not ontologically, then methodologically valid, and can still be used as instruments serving his purpose. Derrida rejects the claim that Lévi-Strauss makes in *Elementary Structures* that the distinction between nature and culture, while of no historical significance, contains a logic, justifying its use by modern sociology as a methodological tool. In Derrida's opinion, to exploit the relative efficacy of these terms in order to destroy the old machinery to which they belong, and of which they are themselves pieces, is by definition a self-defeating project.

But it could easily be argued that the logic Lévi-Strauss intuits in this opposition can yield more fruitful results than the rigorous and systematic logic of Derrida's deconstruction. The logic Lévi-Strauss speaks of is that of myth. As Derrida notices at once, Lévi-Strauss begins as an empirical observer, but ends by accepting the possibility that his investigation may be no more than a myth. It is not immediately apparent, then, why Derrida should spend so much time on deconstructing a writer who has already deconstructed himself? Lévi-Strauss had already stepped beyond narrow regimes

---

[12] Lena Petrovic, 'Remembering and Dismembering: Derrida's Reading of Lévi-Strauss,' *Linguistics and Literature,* Vol. 3, No. 1, 2004, pp. 87–96.

of rationality and rigid empiricism, and moved into the realm of the mythic, or of interpretation and judgement.

Let us now turn to the differing conceptions of reason, the second issue that sets Sartre and Lévi-Strauss at odds with each other. For Sartre, there is a distinction between analytic reason and dialectical reason that places them in tension each with the other. Lévi-Strauss, on the other hand, sees them as being interdependent. In this, too, he follows Kant. For Kant, logic can be separated into two strands—logic of the general—what is analytic logic for Sartre—and logic of the particular—or dependent logic—in the use of understanding. The first contains the necessary laws of reasoning without which no understanding is possible and it operates without regard to the different objects to which it might be applied. The logic of the particular use of reason, on the other hand, deals with the rules of understanding brought to a specific class of objects within a determinate domain. The first is what we might call elemental logic and the second is an organon that makes sense of this or that richly developed science, or other bodies of knowledge.

Analytic reason for Sartre operates independently of dialectical reason regardless of whether we take the relation between them to be oppositional or complementary. For Lévi-Strauss, on the other hand, following Kant fairly strictly on this, dialectical reason is constituted through the operation of both general, or analytic logic, as well as the use of dependent logic. In his words:

> In my view dialectical reason is always constitutive, it is the bridge forever extended and improved, which analytic reason throws over an abyss; it is unable to see the further shore but it knows that it is there, even should it be constantly receding. The term dialectical reason thus covers the perceptual efforts analytical reason must make to reform itself if it aspires to account for language, society and thought; and the distinction between the

two forms of reason on my view rests on the temporary gap separating analytical reason from the understanding of life.[13]

Perhaps there is no clearer expression of the way in which analytic and dialectical, or relational reason, have come to be opposed, than to witness the bitter rejection of analytic reason by some discourses of anti-colonial, anti-patriarchal and other forms of social dominance and oppression. That such rejection rests on a philosophical mistake is also made very clear by Lévi-Strauss, following Kantian logic. There is no way of developing a dependent logic, or a logic that arises organically in relation to a particular set of circumstances, without relying on more general principles of reasoning. Similarly, it is impossible to develop these general principles of reasoning—in a true sense—without engagement with these, and other particular circumstances. In sum, Sartre, seeing analytic and dialectical reason as distinct, comes to reject analytic reason, calling it reason in repose. Lévi-Strauss, on the other hand, following Kant, recognizes that reason is always dialectical—its analytic elements seeking through engagement with particular circumstances to arrive at intermediary conclusions that, in turn, serve as the premises for further exploration and engagement.

Lévi-Strauss, then, returns us to the philosophy of Kant and Merleau-Ponty. He provides us with excellent arguments for steering a course between rationalism and empiricism. We should find it profitable to read him in a time when we have fallen into a sort of radical empiricism in our efforts to step away from the strict norms of rationalism that preceded post-structural critique. Such a returning to the philosophical commitments of Lévi-Strauss would also help us sort through genuine criticism of his thought from those that result from a misunderstanding, or even ignorance, of these commitments. Most importantly, for me, it signals a return to reading

---

[13] Lévi-Strauss, *The Savage Mind*, p. 246.

Kant's philosophy in the non-Cartesian manner that it deserves. Above all, however, we can only profit from placing philosophy and anthropology, thought and experience, in a constitutive rather than oppositional relation. Research from a global perspective places a Kantian demand on us to recognize the constitutive nature of our minds, the structures of thinking and representations that we share as humans with their shared neurological, albeit plastic architecture, and our interconnected histories. In Lévi-Strauss's words, we need to understand more deeply the systems of differences and similarities within which we live our own lives and share those of others, or we run the risk, as Merleau Ponty warns us, of arriving at epistemological judgements that are blind intuitions or empty concepts.

On Language and the Assumed Unity of the Human Sciences

Franson Manjali

At the outset, I wish to state that I shall be dealing primarily with Lévi-Strauss' treatment of language and linguistics, especially in relation to his project of instituting and developing the 'sciences of man'. I would like to begin by referring to certain significant events in my own intellectual life and acknowledge a few individuals with whom I have in some ways formed a sort of invisible kinship in relation to Lévi-Strauss. The latter set in fact, consists, not of anthropologists, but of Professors deeply involved in problems of language and linguistics. They are my colleague and one of the participants here, Harjeet Singh Gill, Professor Emeritus at Jawaharlal Nehru University; Bernard Pottier, my professor at University of Paris-4 (Sorbonne) during 1987–89, and currently a Member-Secretary at the Institut de France, and therefore a working colleague of Lévi-Strauss till the latter's demise last year; and Jean-Petitot, a mathematician and philosopher at École des Hautes Etudes en Sciences Sociales, Paris, who is an unrelenting admirer and follower of the naturalistic and mathematicising project of Lévi-Straussian human sciences.

My own interest in anthropology goes back to 1973 when, still a student of the natural sciences in Calicut, I bought for myself a paperback volume of Margaret Mead's *Anthropology—A Human Science*. (It is perhaps worth mentioning here that Lévi-Strauss was never entirely convinced by the work of this American anthropologist.) On reading the book, I remember being fascinated by the field, especially by a chapter called 'Warfare: An Invention—Not a Biological Necessity'.[1] I cited a passage from this chapter in an article, my first ever, entitled 'Down with Wars' in a publication that appeared the following year. I shall re-cite it here:

> ...there are peoples even today who have no warfare. Of these the Eskimos are perhaps the most conspicuous example, but the Lepchas of Sikkim are an equally good one. Neither of these peoples understand war, not even the defensive warfare. The idea of warfare is lacking, and this idea is as essential to carrying on war as an alphabet or a syllabary to writing.[2]

Along with my incessant longing for a world free of wars, and my silent admiration for the two warless peoples of the world, what began then as a fleeting fascination for anthropology—perhaps my first academic romance—continued for a long time since my fortuitous first encounter with Mead's book. A few years later in Delhi, I borrowed a copy of Lévi-Strauss's *Structural Anthropology* from Dr Abhilasha Kumari, a Sociologist from Jawaharlal Nehru University (JNU). When I went to return the book to her a couple of years later, Abhilasha was indeed so kind as to convert this loan into a gift. Although, I had read this book only in bits and pieces, I have always guarded it as a valuable treasure. Apart from its academic value, my current possession of the book pleases me for somewhat different reasons. The book was bought (possibly by Abhilasha

---

[1] This was a journal paper, originally published in 1940.

[2] Margaret Mead, *Anthropology: A Human Science*, New Delhi: East-West Press, 1964, p.127.

herself, for her name is inscribed in red ball-point ink on the first page) from a second-hand bookshop called 'Hobby Corner' at 4L Hazrat Gunj in Lucknow. The last page of the book prominently bears the black seal of the Hobby Corner, and on the inner front cover there is the name of its possible first owner and the date of purchase, written in black ink of a fountain-pen: 'Wm Heavey, December 1967, Amherst.' As you can see, one is delighted at this fund of sociological information of other places, times and people, which can invoke the imagination and interest of a bibliophile, or perhaps vice-versa.

By the time I bought Volume 2 of Lévi-Strauss's *Structural Anthropology* in October 1981 (my copy bears this date), I had already developed a somewhat active interest in cultural anthropology by way of an optional course called 'Culture, Society and Personality,' that I did as an MA student at the Centre for the Study of Social Systems at JNU. This course opened my eyes to the significance and the possibility of applying Linguistics—a field in which I did my master's and doctoral degrees without ever being fully convinced of its dominant formalist enterprise—in the social sciences. This was a great relief, because it meant that even after having espoused the so-called scientific discipline of Linguistics, one could continue one's first, albeit fleeting, relationship with Antrhopology. I was even more delighted to read at some point Lévi-Strauss's forceful endorsement of and emphasis on the use of linguistic ideas and methods in Anthropology. Thanks to Lévi-Strauss, and following a trajectory contrary to his, I was readily convinced that if Linguistics had any use at all, it was in its application in the Social Sciences, especially Anthropology. Having been a student of the natural sciences at the Bachelor's level, desiring to traverse the scientific ambitions of linguistics, and still seeking to avert a wholesale intellectual disenchantment, the following words of Lévi-Strauss provided me, if not with elation, then at least with a glimmer of hope of being able to explore outside one's own 'discipline': 'Structural linguistics will certainly play the same renovating role with respect to the social sciences that nuclear physics, for example, has played for the physical sciences.'[3]

I must note here that although this prediction has been subsequently belied, it did not prevent me from calling my first book, with a certain Lévi-Straussian tenor *Nuclear Semantics— Towards a Theory of Relational Meaning*.[4] I must also note here that at the beginning of the chapter that contains the above citation, Lévi-Strauss expresses his overwhelming enthusiasm for the field of my specialization:

> Linguistics occupies a special place among the social sciences, to whose ranks it unquestionably belongs. It is not merely a social science like the others, but rather, the one in which by far the greatest progress has been made. It is probably the one which can truly claim to be a science and which has achieved both the formulation of an empirical method and an understanding of the nature of the data submitted to its analysis.[5]

Ever since I read these lines in the early 1980s, I have paid sustained and serious attention to these ultimately not-so-prophetic words of Lévi-Strauss concerning the relevance of Structural Linguistics (and later, its near-antagonistic counterpart, post-structuralism) in the social sciences as well as in cultural and literary studies. This orientation of mine became even more pronounced after Professor Gill joined Jawaharlal Nehru University in late 1984. A lot of what I have done in my own academic career—even

---

[3] C. Lévi-Strauss, *Structural Anthropology*, (tr.) Claire Jacobson. New York: Anchor Books. Chapter II, 'Structural Analysis in Linguistics and Anthropology', p. 31.

[4] Bahri Publications, New Delhi, 1991. This book is largely based on my post-doctoral work in Paris from 1987 to 1989 in association with B. Pottier and J. Petitot.

[5] C. Lévi-Strauss, *Structural Anthropology*, op. cit., p. 28.

when it was sometimes against his convictions—owes itself to the fortunate relationship I could develop with Professor Gill, first as an informal student and later as a colleague and friend whose views I respected, in the Centre for Linguistics and English at Jawaharlal Nehru University.

Thanks to Gill, the world of structuralism and semiotics on the one hand, and to a lesser extent Sartrean existentialism on the other, opened up before my eyes. Soon, apart from Lévi-Strauss, the other French philosophers or 'theoreticians'—I use this Anglo-Saxon academic term with a certain amusement today—Lacan, Althusser, Barthes, Sartre, Merleau-Ponty, Greimas, Todorov and Kristeva became household names. (By this time, however, the names of the post-structuralist philosophers, Foucault and Derrida, had begun to appear on our intellectual horizon through separate student networks.) The question of existence and signification and their mutual relationship had begun to pervade every field that one exposed oneself to. In the process, the Anglo-American field of a (mere) formalized Semantics which one studied as part of the Linguistics programme, and around which I wrote a doctoral thesis, began to recede into the background and the French field of Semiotics and related domains emerged in its place.

With hindsight, I can now say that what whetted my appetite during this period was Lévi-Strauss's insistence that social facts are representations, and his invention of the 'human sciences' where Anthropology would have a central role, and whose methodological systematization and deepening would require Linguistics and Semiotics. We know that the Swiss-French linguist Ferdinand de Saussure had proposed Semiology as an overarching discipline that studies the 'life of signs in society' based on the core principles of Linguistics. We also know that for Lévi-Strauss, there were in fact two different moments when structural linguistics was sought to be made the methodological foundation of Anthropology in the creation of the human sciences. The *first* of these involved incorporating into Anthropology the theory of 'distinctive features' in phonology initially propounded by the Russian linguists Nikolai Trubetzkoy and Roman Jakobson working under the rubric of the Prague Linguistic Circle, and which Lévi-Strauss had learned from the latter during his sojourn in New York during the 1940s. Though the attractive analogy between phonology and 'nuclear physics' must have been exaggerated, what mattered was the idea that the lowest analytical elements of the two domains, the atom and the phoneme, can be further broken down into sub-atomic particles or sub-phonemeic binary features ('pairs of oppositions') respectively. What was important for Lévi-Strauss, however, is that the atom or the phoneme forms part of 'systems', physical in the first, and 'unconscious' mental in the second. By way of extension of this idea, the 'atoms of kinship' form 'unconscious' systems of society: 'Like phonemes, kinship terms are elements of meaning; like phonemes, they acquire meaning only if they are integrated into systems.' Kinship systems,' like 'phonemic systems,' are built by the mind on the level of the unconscious thought.'[6]

Lévi-Strauss' three-fold fascination for structural linguistics is clearly expressed in the above sentence: the shift from a study of conscious phenomena to that of their *unconscious* substructure; the shift from terms to *relations*; and the emphasis on *system*.[7]

---

[6] Ibid., p. 32. Lévi-Strauss clarifies this analogy further: 'We know that to obtain a structural law the linguist analyses phonemes into "distinctive features", which he can then group into one or several "pairs of oppositions". Following an analogous method, the anthropologist might be tempted to break down analytically the kinship terms of any given system into components... the term *father* has positive connotations with respect to sex, relative age, and generation; but it has a zero value on the dimension of collaterality, and it cannot express an affinal relationship'" (ibid., p. 33).

[7] Ibid., p. 31.

The *second* moment, almost simultaneously with the first, was his definition of 'social anthropology' in terms of its equivalence with Saussure's 'Semiology.' The basis of this equivalence is Lévi-Strauss' observation that '(f)or anthropology, which is a conversation of man with man, all things are symbol and sign which act as intermediaries between two subjects.'[8] Saussure on his part had viewed language as a 'social institution' which is based in the collective psyche of a society. In his conception of an ordered chain of the human sciences, Linguistics, or the science of language, is a part, albeit the defining one, of Semiology, the 'science that studies life of signs in society,' which is in turn a part of 'social psychology,' itself a branch of psychology.

Thus, in his *leçon inaugurale* at Collège de France in January 1960, Lévi-Strauss forcefully announced the affinity and even the equivalence between 'social anthropology' and 'semiology'. Posing himself the question, 'What, then, is social anthropology?' he answered:

> Although he did not specifically name it, Ferdinand de Saussure came very close to defining it when he introduced linguistics as part of a science yet to be born, for which he reserved the name 'semiology'. Its object of study he saw to be the life of signs at the heart of social life. Did he not, furthermore foresee our adherence when he compared language to 'writing, to alphabet of deaf-mutes, to symbolic rites, to forms of politeness, to military signals, etc.'? No one would deny that anthropology includes in its own field at least some of these systems of signs, to which it adds many others, such as mythical language, the oral and gestural signs of which ritual is composed, marriage rules, kinship systems, customary laws, and certain forms of economic exchange.[9]

---

[8] C. Lévi-Strauss, *Structural Anthropology 2*, (tr.) Monique Layton. Harmondsworth: Penguin, 1973. Chapter I, 'The Scope of Anthropology,' Monique Layton, p. 11.

[9] C. Lévi-Strauss, ibid., p. 9. The inset quotation is from F. de Saussure, *Course in*

It is worth noting here that it was on the basis of Lévi-Strauss' work and his pronouncements that structuralism and *semiologie* (more popularly 'semiotics,' based on an Anglo-Saxon conception of the field) rose to a position of prominence in the French intellectual context in the 1950s and the first half of the 1960s.[10] We can find elements of structuralism and semiotics in the works of some of the major French thinkers of the period: Maurice Merleau-Ponty, Jacques Lacan, Fernand Braudel, Louis Althusser, and particularly Roland Barthes who went on to publish a book called *Eléménts de la Sémiologie* in 1964, and was later appointed as the Professor of Semiology in Collège de France in 1977. We can also see that Lévi-Strauss was the main inspiration behind Professor Gill's founding a department of Anthropological Linguistics at the University of Patiala, in the Punjab, and later leading a research programme in Semiotics at JNU from 1984 to 2001, the year of his retirement.[11] It is also clearly a Lévi-Straussian inspiration that prompted the present author to introduce an MPhil Course called *Linguistics and Human Sciences* as a part of JNU's Semiotics programme in 1992.

Lévi-Strauss' articulation of the relation between language and culture at three different levels has been of particular interest to me. The first of these is the relation between a particular language and the corresponding (particular) culture. The point here is that the knowledge of a language and that of a culture can be reciprocally productive. The second has to do with the way in which cultures treat language and conversely how an awareness of culture is encompassed in languages. Lévi-Strauss is more inclined to favour a third level of relation which is 'the relation between linguistics as

General Linguistics, Glasgow: Fontana Classics, 1969, p. 16.

[10] Structuralism had become outmoded in France by the time of the May '68 movement.

[11] We note here that this rich and fertile academic programme was discontinued at Jawaharlal Nehru University a few years after Gill's retirement.

a scientific discipline and anthropology'.[12] In addition to the usual inclusive relations of either language being a product of culture, or an inclusive part of culture, Lévi-Strauss insists on language being a 'condition of culture'. Here again, it is not just the necessity of language for the acquisition of culture that Lévi-Strauss is insisting on, but rather the analogical relation between a theoretically-identifiable material of language and the material of culture.

> ... from a ... theoretical point of view; language can be said to be the *condition of culture* because the material out of which language is built is of the same type as the material out of which the whole culture is built: *logical relations, oppositions, correlations,* and the like. Language, from this point of view, may appear as laying a kind of foundation for the more complex structures which correspond to the different aspects of culture.[13]

Through my own interest in a semiotics of narrative, the area of Lévi-Strauss's work that I followed more closely is his structuralist analysis of myths and folktales. In 1958, Lévi-Strauss wrote an influential review of the Russian folklorist Vladimir Propp's work from a strictly structuralist perspective, criticizing the latter's formalist paradigm.[14] In proposing his own method of analysing myths and tales, he highlighted the semantic and contextual aspects which were mostly to be identified in the specific use of vocabulary.

Here too, as in his analysis of kinship, Lévi-Strauss has pointed out the usefulness of the Prague school theory of distinctive features based on the principle of binary oppositions. Further, Lévi-Strauss

---

[12] C. Lévi-Strauss, 'Linguistics and Anthropology', *Structural Anthropology*, op. cit., p. 67.

[13] Ibid., p. 67.

[14] C. Lévi-Strauss, 'Structure and Form: Reflections on a Work of Vladimir Propp.' Chapter VIII of *Structural Anthropology 2*, op. cit., pp. 115–45. The reference work is Vladimir Propp, *Morphology of the Folktale*. (tr.) Lawrence Scott. Austin: University of Texas Press, 1968.

argues that instead of describing the structure of the folktale, Propp had reduced it to its bare formal framework. Structure, in his view, cannot be divorced from content: 'Structure has no distinct content; it is content itself, apprehended in a logical organization as a property of the real.'[15]

Propp's tendency to view 'functions' alone as relevant (on the basis of their being constant) and the terms that support this function as arbitrary, is severely criticized. For Lévi-Strauss, it is the vocabulary that conveys specific structural content, both in relation to historical and ethnographic information, and in terms of the relevant oppositions that is significant within the context of a given folktale. For formalism, Lévi-Strauss concludes, 'form alone is intelligible, and content is only a residual, deprived of any significant value.' While for structuralism, 'there is not something abstract on one side and concrete on the other. Form and content are of the same nature, susceptible to the same analysis. Content draws its reality from its structure and what is called form is the "structural formation" of the local structure forming the content.'[16]

The terms that are part of a function cannot be considered 'variable', because they do have a value in the context where the tale occurs. The terms for the characters may have universal validity, but often they are relative to the social context. For example, a plum tree and an apple tree have different values, since the former is recognized for its 'fecundity' while the latter is known for the 'strength and depth of its roots'. As a consequence, instead of viewing the characters perform a function as arbitrary, they have to be seen in their specific value defined positively (for instance, 'fecundity' in the former) or negatively (for instance, 'earth-sky transition'

---

[15] C. Lévi-Strauss, 'Structure and Form: Reflections on Work by Vladimir Propp', *Structural Anthropology 2*, op. cit., p. 115.

[16] Ibid., p. 131.

in the latter). Plus, in this case both have the 'vegetal' feature in common. Thus, Lévi-Strauss notes, 'a "universe of the tale" will be progressively defined, analysable in pairs of oppositions, diversely combined within each character—which far from constituting a single entity—is a bundle of differential elements, in the manner of the phoneme as conceived by Roman Jakobson.'[17] Lévi-Strauss employs in his analysis a set of binary opposites like nature vs. culture, life vs. death, endogamy vs. exogamy, male vs. female, high vs. low, earth vs. sky, day vs. night, animal vs. vegetal, and so on.

Following the same principle of 'differential oppositions' or distinctive features, Lévi-Strauss suggests a systematic reduction in the number of Propp's 31 functions. For instance, the functions of 'violation', 'prohibition' and 'injunction' can all be grouped together as one or the other transformation of the same function. Accordingly, 'violation' would be the reverse of 'prohibition' and the latter a negative transformation of the 'injunction'. Similarly, 'departure' of the hero and his 'return' could be considered as the same function of disjunction, positively or negatively defined. The 'search' by the hero would be the converse of his 'pursuit', and so on.[18]

Evidently, Lévi-Strauss finds it hard to accept Propp's conception of a grammar of the narrative which does not pay any attention to the specific use of vocabulary and its contextual signification. Even when drawing from a universal set of binary semantic features, the words possess culturally rooted connotations which it is the job of an ethnographer to identify. It is this 'second power' of words (i.e., functioning as metaphors/metonyms) employed in the narrative that reveal the structural content of the myths and tales.

---

[17] Ibid., p. 135.
[18] Ibid., p. 137.

Following Lévi-Strauss, Greimas in his *Structural Semantics*[19] attempted a grand formalization of the narrative content. Here the latter adopted Lévi-Strauss' idea that the narrative 'functions' can be understood as transformations, on the basis of which Greimas introduced the concept of the 'semiotic square' which while being a development of the concept of binary oppositions, is introduced to reveal the more complex articulations of a semic category in terms of relations of contrariness, contradiction and implication. Semiotic square is defined as the 'visual representation of the logical articulation of any category'[20] (Greimas and Courtés, 1979: 29).

Evidently, it is indeed a mathematicisable structural logic of language that Lévi-Strauss places his whole faith in. If, in spite of a range of common interests and concerns shared between linguistics and anthropology, the former has theoretically overtaken the latter, it is because, Lévi-Strauss believes, linguistics has more rapidly adopted the methods of the natural sciences. He exhorts himself and fellow anthropologists 'to learn from the linguists' and to be able to use the latter's 'rigorous' and by far 'successful' approach. Curiously, linguists and anthropologists have sought each other for contradictory reasons. They have even gone after each other in an 'unhappy merry-go-around'—the linguists trying to acquire from anthropology the feature of concreteness for their observation and data, and the anthropologists trying to systematize the abundance of their concrete data. In Lévi-Strauss' figurative formulation, linguistics provided the tiny door for approaching the paradise of the natural and exact sciences which scholars in the social and human sciences had thought they could never enter.[21]

---

[19] A.J. Greimas, *Structural Semantics*, (tr.) D. McDowell, R. Schleifer and A. Velie. Lincoln: University of Nebraska Press, 1983.

[20] A.J. Greimas and J. Courtés, *Sémiotique: Dictionnaire raisonné de la théorie du langage*. Paris: Hachette, 1979.

[21] Ibid., pp. 68–69.

It is not difficult to recognize that Lévi-Strauss, a contemporary of some of the most well-known French thinkers of the twentieth century, namely, Sartre, Lévinas, Blanchot, de Beauvoir and Merleau-Monty (all five of them were born between 1905 and 1908, and are now deceased) was the principal figure behind the formation of a distinctly French field of the *sciences de l'homme*, whose founder, according to Lévi-Strauss, was none other than the eighteenth-century social philosopher, Jean-Jacques Rousseau. Like Rousseau, Lévi-Strauss dreamt of making the empirical 'man', the anthropological 'man', the centre of philosophy. It was from Rousseau, he says he learnt the one and 'only' principle on which to base the sciences of man: 'To attain acceptance of oneself in others (the goal assigned to human knowledge by the ethnologist), one must first deny the self in oneself.'[22] According to Lévi-Strauss, it is neither abstract knowledge nor a Cartesian self-doubt, but an ethnographic exposure to the other in the process of which one may renounce one's own self-knowledge, and deny all other cherished knowledge and ideals—this is what constitutes the philosophical attitude of an anthropologist. In this sense, the anthropologist is a 'spontaneous' philosopher.

Despite this dalliance with philosophy, linguistics, with its simultaneous treatment of form and meaning and its emphasis on unconscious structure, remained for Lévi-Strauss, his principal orientation. Elements of kinship and other aspects and artefacts of culture can be expressed as relations, and they have a *meaning* for human beings. Therefore, they can be treated as *signs*—even 'a stone axe can be a sign'—which for the specific system can be on par with the signs system of language. The nature of these relations and the system of their meanings are not evident to the members

---

[22] C. Lévi-Strauss, 'Jean-Jacques Rousseau, Founder of the Sciences of Man', *Structural Anthropology 2,* op. cit., p. 36.

of the society, because they exist only at an *unconscious* plane of the human mind, but they can be studied by the anthropologist by means of his rigorous methods. What the structural analysis reveals are the universal structures of the unconscious human mind, which manifests differently in specific customs, practices and discourses, but which are related to each other in terms of rules of permutation, combination and other transformation. On the basis of a belief in such unconscious universal structures, Lévi-Strauss is keen to annul the dichotomy between the savage and the civilized man as well as between synchrony and diachrony. 'In anthropology as in linguistics, … the synchronic can be as unconscious as the diachronic. In this sense … the divergence between the two is reduced.'[23] Further, the structures that encompass both history and society, that is, the structures of the human sciences, would be, from Lévi-Strauss' point of view, part of more general naturalistic structures. All phenomena and all structures can thus be naturalized and understood in terms of mutual transformations within a single form. In order to express this ultimate dream of the mathematician, Lévi-Strauss refers us to Goethe:

> All forms are similar, and none is like the others.
> So that their chorus points the way to a hidden law.[24]

As for me, I had sought, from my early undergraduate days, following a contrary trajectory, to escape from the natural sciences

---

[23] C. Lévi-Strauss, 'The Scope of Anthropology,' ibid., p. 17.

[24] Quoted in C. Lévi-Strauss, ibid., p. 18. This statement suggesting a Goethean foundation of a naturalistic (topologico-dynamic) structuralism receives an elaborate treatment in a recent work by Jean Petitot: *Morphologie et Esthétique*, Paris: Maisonneuve et Larose, 2004. Lévi-Strauss' own naturalist inclinations originated in his childhood fascination for geology. He says: 'I count among my most precious memories … a hike along the flank of a limestone plateau in Languedoc to determine the lien of contact between two geological strata.' (C. Lévi-Strauss, 'The Making of an Anthropologist', *Tristes Tropiques*, (tr.) John and Doreen Weightman, Harmondsworth: Penguin, 1978, p. 68.)

into some sort of a philosophical paradise through the tiny door that anthropology seemed to offer me. Since then I have never been keen to return to any field of natural sciences, despite several intimations of it. And ever since I familiarized myself with the intellectual currents that constitute post-structuralism and postmodernism during my stay as a fellow at the Indian Institute of Advanced Study in Shimla during the late 1990s, I have turned away from Lévi-Straussian anthropology. During this period and later, I have been particularly influenced by a critique of the 'human sciences' based at least in part on a Nietzschean perspective coming from Foucault and Derrida.

As early as his *leçon inaugurale* of 1960, Lévi-Strauss was aware of some of the criticisms that were being directed at the social anthropologist, and he chose to refute them. He refutes the charge of anthropology being an offshoot of colonialism, by stating that it is through the latter that the former has been able to develop a pan-human dimension, that is, 'to extend humanism to the measure of humanity'.[25] But, as the critics of anthropology have insisted, the problem is essentially this: how can man be both the subject and object of a science. The task of Foucault's *Les mots et les choses—Une Archéologie des Sciences Humaines* is to study the historical emergence of man in his double capacity of a subject and an object of the human sciences. Unlike Lévi-Strauss, Foucault does not believe that the human sciences came into existence as part of a historical continuity of human reason when the latter included man as an object of enquiry. But rather, according to Foucault, human sciences 'appeared when man constituted himself in Western culture as both that which must be conceived of and that which must be known'. In other words, human sciences emerged as a specific discursive formation with its own objects and rules of analysis. According to

---

[25] C. Lévi-Strauss, *Structural Anthropology 2*, op. cit., p. 32.

Foucault's archeological analysis, 'man is only a recent invention, a figure not yet two centuries old, a new wrinkle in our knowledge, and ... will disappear again as soon as that knowledge has discovered a new form.'[26] As for ethnology, Foucault, expressing his misgivings in tune with other post-structuralists (and post-colonialists) observes that it is a field that 'can assume its proper dimensions only within the historical sovereignty—always restrained, but always present—of European thought and the relation that can bring it face to face with all other cultures as well as with itself.'[27]

Derrida's initial critique of Lévi-Strauss, more direct than that of Foucault, is in the form of a conference paper presented in 1966 at Baltimore in the United States. It is centrally concerned with the problem of structure.[28] The problem of structure is in fact the problem of its centre, or rather, the centring authority. Lévi-Strauss' insistence on naturalistic human sciences, Derrida attempts to show, is based on his adherence to a binary opposition—fundamental in western culture—between nature and culture, even when it is faced with the 'scandal' concerning incest prohibition which can be deemed as both natural and cultural. Even when Lévi-Strauss exalts the natural 'innocence' of the primitive peoples, he is well entrenched within the dominant philosophies of the west and its languages which centrally bear the foundational opposition between nature and culture. His decision to support primitive

[26] M. Foucault, *The Order of Things: An Archaeology of the Human Sciences* (translated from the French of *Les mots et les choses*). London: Tavistock, 1966/1970. pp. 344–45.

[27] Ibid., p. 377.

[28] Jacques Derrida, 'Structure, Sign and Play in the Discourse of the Human Sciences', in Chapter 10 in *Writing and Difference*, (tr.) Alan Bass. London: Routledge, pp. 278-93. For another instance of his critique of Lévi-Strauss, see Part II, I, 'The Violence of the Letter: From Lévi-Strauss to Rousseau,' in J. Derrida, *Of Grammatology*, (tr.) G. Chakravorty-Spivak, Delhi: Motilal Banarasidass, 1967/1976. pp. 101–40.

'nature' against western 'culture,' à la Rousseau, itself proceeds from a determination to arrest the 'play' inherent (and evident, even for Lévi-Strauss!) in any structure, and thus impose on the observational field of ethnology the power of the western science. In a key paragraph in his 'Structure, Sign and Play in the Discourse of the Human Sciences', Derrida rejects Lévi-Strauss' plea that structural 'totalization' of the ethnographic domain turns out to be impossible (in spite of the anthropologist's best intentions and efforts) because of the vastness and the unending nature of the ethnographic field and data. He argues instead that this impossibility is because

> ... the nature of the field, that is language, a finite language, excludes totalization. This field is in effect that of *play*, that is to say a field of infinite substitutions only because it is finite, that is to say, because instead of being an inexhaustive field, as in classical hypothesis, instead of being too large, there is something missing from it, namely, a centre which arrests and grounds the play of substitutions.... this movement of play, permitted by the lack or absence of a centre or origin, is the movement of *supplementarity*. One cannot determine the centre and exhaust totalization because the sign which replaces the centre, which supplements it, taking the centre's place in its absence—this sign is added, occurs as a surplus, as a *supplement*.[29]

Thus, in the context of our awareness of the absent origin or absent centre, there can be two contrary versions of interpretations—ethnographic or linguistic—according to Derrida. One is Rousseauistic: 'sad, *negative*, nostalgic, guilty;' the other is Nietzschean, characterized by '*affirmation*, that is the joyous affirmation of the play of the world and of the innocence of becoming, the affirmation of a world of signs without fault, without truth, and without origin which is offered to an active interpretation.'[30]

---

[29] J. Derrida, 'Structure, Sign and Play...' op. cit., p. 289.
[30] Ibid., p. 292.

'Naming' Conversion
Being Muslim in Old Delhi

DEEPAK MEHTA

In *Narrating Lives*, Metcalf (2004: 340–48) shows how a distinctive Indo-Persian topos links the self to the world. She isolates three significant characteristics of this topos: (*a*) chronology is irrelevant since the narrated self resonates with an essence and life stories are told as episodes that are 'not causally or developmentally linked' (ibid.: 343); (*b*) the self thus documented represents timeless patterns— 'significance is found in similarity, not difference' (ibid.: 344); (*c*) the self is imagined as responding to external events, being embedded in networks and relationships. In recognizing that life stories, though fictive, highlight valued activities of cultures, Metcalf presents such accounts as stable elaborations, where visions and the movement of the inexplicable in changing the course of one's life, are firmly rooted in established interpretive communities. The arguments of this essay are somewhat more unruly than Metcalf's restrained and sustained analyses of Muslim movements and histories of North India. Exploring a narrative of religious conversion, I argue that the interpretive communities within which the conversion experience is located, are bundles of intersecting and often contradictory discourses, affects and practices. Conversion, in this sense is not so much a movement into a single and stable community of belief, as it is an attempt to establish the limits of interpretation. While these limits cannot be fitted under a single explanatory regime, we find, however, that within the limits there is a range of meanings associated with the term 'Muslim'.[1] As part of the conversion story, the name Muslim is linked to a 'pure language', in the way that Lévi-Strauss (1987) uses this term, but also to social relationships in everyday life, marked by emotion, impulse and sensation. This essay is an attempt to establish the link between naming and a pure language.

In this essay I focus on the conversion experience of Ahmad Khan, a former communist turned member of the *Ahl-e-Hadith* (Peoples of Tradition, hereafter AH), who stays in a neighbourhood known as Ballimaran in the walled city of Delhi, and with whom I have been in intermittent conversation since July 2006.[2] In charting his movement from communism to an orthodox version of Islam, I carry out two sorts of investigations. The first shows how the term 'Muslim' moves across various arenas of social life, ranging from its

---

[1] Far from providing a general model of conversion, the essay argues that the practices of being a 'good Muslim' are invariably affected by sources and contexts. In this sense, it does not argue for a pristine Islam. Two background assumptions frame the essay. The first follows Alam's view (2004: 3–4) that Islam in the subcontinent is an 'alloy'. He notes that an alloyed Islam pre-dated its entry into the Indian subcontinent. Sometimes the alloy intersected with local traditions, at other times it established hierarchies within an Islam that accommodated local traditions (ibid.: 163–64). Second, if conversion into this alloy points to a current orthodoxy, the essay holds, along with Asad (1986: 15) that such orthodoxy is a reflex of power, where moments of exchange and conflict complicate a monolithic narrative of Islamic orthodoxy. Individual actors and narrators need to be read in terms of an open-ended process where networked exchanges reinforce established norms and orthodoxies, even as they submit them to challenge.

[2] Together with my co-worker, Rumman Hameed, we began fieldwork in Ballimaran in June 2006 by walking through three neighbourhoods—Punjabi Phatak, Gali Qasimjan and Kucha Rehman.

incarnation as a word that has almost revelatory significance, to its embedding in material and social relations. For example, 'Muslim' in Khan's didactic understanding of conversion appears to be a term that has purely ritual meaning. Here, he highlights visions and dreams (what he calls *ru'ya*) in shaping a narrative of the self. From the point of view of his everyday and material life, his way of being Muslim is conditioned by his interactions with those who are of different persuasion. In this context, to be Muslim is linked to 'doing what is right', but also to securing a livelihood. Sometimes the term 'Muslim' is used to resolve domestic crises, revealing also a secret and illicit knowledge of social relations. Here, the material objects associated with this term, such as the *tawiz* (amulet, charm), are sometimes invested with potent forces, influencing the people who come into contact with them. Thus, particular discursive forms, affects and material objects mediate the term, one where the use of ambiguity is often emphasiszd.

In making sense of Khan's conversion the ethnography reveals a tension between those who are members of the AH and non-AH Muslims. This tension is grounded in a morality that is part of a programme of reform of the AH. Khan claims that through their utterances and embodied practices, men and women members of the AH become bearers of this morality. In turn, this moralizing force allows us to envision the way in which the AH has assumed the right to define orthodoxy. This right places all other Islamic doctrines as formal heresies, i.e., a 'wilful persistence in error' (Jackson: 3). Heresy overlaps with several categories of deviance, from unbelief (*kufr*) to unsanctioned innovation (*bid'a*), to genuine misunderstandings. Drawing from the experiences of his life, Khan advocates invitation (*daw'at*) as a way of addressing and overcoming unbelief. But under this daw'at lies the uneasy emergence of the AH as a singular theo-political category.

Ahl-e-Hadith

There are no standard works on the AH, though references are often made to this movement, mainly to offset either the Deoband seminary and school of thought (Metcalf 1982; Zaman 2002) or the Barelwi movement (Sanyal 1999; new edition 2010).[3] Emerging in India in the second half of the nineteenth century, the AH distinguished itself from the Deobandis and Barelwis in significant ways. Like them, it affirms its reverence for the teachings of the Prophet, but it differs in its understanding of the sources of religious authority. The Barelwis avow not only the authority of the Prophet but also the teachings of saints and holy people, whom they see as vehicles of mediation between god and human beings (Sanyal 1999). The Deobandis preach against shrine worship and insist on the legitimacy of their Hanafi School of law and on the investiture of authority (*taqlid*) concerning matters agreed upon by this school tradition (Metcalf 1982). In a variety of local religious practices, however, the Deobandis, like the Barelwis, use a *pir-murid* (teacher-student) network to disseminate learning. Formally, the AH deny the legitimacy of all practices lacking a basis in scriptural texts and are implacably opposed to the classical schools of law. The AH insist on the Quran and selected hadith as the exclusive and directly accessible sources of guidance and in this connection

---

[3] Sometimes, AH is used as a synonym for the Salafis. Roy (2004: 234–43) argues that the AH in Pakistan is closely linked to state patronage, a network of religious schools and the *jihad* in Kashmir. In India, the AH seems to be a UFO (unidentified fundamentalist object) in the words of Roy. The Sunnah Islamic Page (http://al-sunnah.com) and Roy provide a detailed web-list of fundamentalist organizations. My unease with these readings is that they establish a strict relation of contemporary institutions and movements to a so-called purist version of Islam, traced to Salafi theology and Wahhabism. In this paper I treat the AH as a sectarian group with local specificities. For Salafism see Duderija (2007: 289–323) and Wiktorowicz (2003: 208–34).

they have produced a corpus of 'authentic' texts. AH scholars were at the forefront of writing and publishing on hadith in the late nineteenth and early twentieth centuries. Zaman (2002:140) notes that like the Wahhabis of the Arabian Peninsula they admired the work of Ibn Taymiyya. Siddiq Hasan Khan was one of the most prominent scholars of the AH. Educated at al-Azhar, he published a variety of texts and had Ibn Hajar's classic commentary on Bukhari's *Sahih* published and widely disseminated (ibid.). The *Sahih* is the reference work for matters religious among the AH of Ballimaran and there are annual prizes awarded to those who can recite, 'by heart', the summarized version. It is used as a kind of dictionary and guidebook for questions concerning orthodoxy and orthopraxy.

In Ballimaran, the AH appear to be divided over the tactics to be used in the promotion of their doctrine. One branch, by far the predominant one, advocates personal and communal religious transformation through lessons, sermons, education and other instruments of propagation (*da'wat*). Its activities are directed towards convincing Muslims of different persuasions of the folly of their views. A second, and smaller strain of the AH is made up of those who do not attempt to persuade. Instead, they maintain a distance from other Muslims in matters concerning prayer and doctrine. Khan belongs to this second group, while his wife belongs to the first.

The AH has a mosque made up of three floors in Ballimaran. Men pray on the ground floor while women pray on the upper floors. The mosque has two entrances. The main entrance opens up to the men's section and leads through a narrow stairway to the upper floors. The second entrance is reserved exclusively for women, opening up from a side door. The call to prayer is initiated by a male caller (*muezzin*) and imam on the ground floor. Women congregate only on Friday in this mosque. During Ramzan the mosque holds *tarawih* (praying at night during Ramzan), which non-AH Muslims offer at home. Usually during Ramzan only the first two *rakaats* are offered in the congregation; those present, men as well as women complete the rest of the *namaaz* on their own. On Fridays, in the AH mosque in Punjabi Phatak, about 30–40 women congregate to offer *namaaz*. Rumman Hameed, my co-worker and a non-AH Muslim offered prayers in this mosque during the Ramzan of 2006. Observing her mode of praying, an old woman admonished her, *oonchi namaaz padha keejiye aap* (read the upper namaz). On being asked the reason, she responded, *kyonki woh hi sahi tareeqa hai. Zameen par sirf saat aza'a tikne chahiye, neechi namaz men to poora jism zameen par tikta hai* (Because that's the right practice. Touch only the seven parts of your body to the ground; in the lower namaz the entire body sticks to the ground). The practice of 'upper namaaz', Rumman was told, was the one advocated by the Prophet. *Huzoor aise hi padhte the, Huzoor ne sab se kaha jaise mein padhta hu, tum bhi waise hi padho, aurto aur mardo ke liye alag tareeqa thodi hoga*. To counter this practice, non-AH Muslim women cite a *hadith* emphasizing that women should offer 'lower namaz' since in the upper namaz there is the danger of immodesty *(oonchi namaz mein bepardagi hoti hai)*.

BALLIMARAN

Chandni Chowk neighbours Ballimaran on the one side, Ahata Kaley Sahab on the other and Chawri Bazar on the third. Ballimaran is a major market for synthetics, footwear, spectacle frames and sunglasses. These shops stretch into Kucha Rehman, a contiguous residential area.[4] Mainly Muslim traders inhabit Ballimaran. They call themselves the *qaum-e-saudagaran* (community of traders) or the *Punjabi saudagaran* (Punjabi traders), and most of them run

---

[4] During Ramzan, Ballimaran changes into a culinary treat in the night, with numerous chefs setting up their makeshift restaurants by the roadside.

small businesses and petty shops often from a part of their own houses. They are also known as *karkhanedars* (owners of workshops). Most names of Punjabi Muslims end with 'waale' (lit: belonging to, of), such as *Ghadiwale* (watch maker, or repairer) or *Jooteywale* (shoe-maker, or more commonly dealer in leather), referring to the business that the family was involved in. The neighbourhood has labourers who work in small workshops, and sometimes live there—bricklayers (*Gadheris*), masons and other manual workers. Members of traditional occupations, such as the night-soil removers (*Halal-Khwor* and *Lalbegi*), cotton carders (*Momin*) and milkmen (*Ghosi*) come from neighbouring Suiwalan and Matia Mahal. A settlement history is difficult to elicit, mainly because of fundamental changes in ownership of immovable property after Partition. What is documented is that in 1947, migrating Muslims from the walled city of Delhi left behind 10,212 houses and industrial premises and 20,198 acres of agricultural land (*Constituent Assembly of India, Legislative Debates, November-December 1949*. Delhi: Manager of Publications, 1949. p. 4). Following the migration, Muslims from other parts of the country illegally occupied mosques, cemeteries and other religious institutional property. In law, vacated properties were indexed under the Evacuee Property Act, but after the 1965 war with Pakistan, the Enemy Property Act replaced the Evacuee Property Act (*Annual Report of the National Minority Commission*, Delhi: National Minorities Commission, 1999). Most of the residents that I talked to in Ballimaran mentioned that their residential properties were de-notified only after 1965, when they were asked to produce documentary proof of usufruct.

A neighbourhood civic organization, known as the Punjabi Anjuman (society) of Ballimaran, carries out a yearly census of the Punjabi traders and often arbitrates in conflicts between neighbours. It is made up of six elected members and functions through donations made by traders. In recent years the AH has had a majority of its members elected to the Anjuman. The Anjuman settles disputes within the community, largely regarding property and marriage issues. The traders prefer to approach the Anjuman than civil courts of law. The Anjuman also brings out a census of the traders, maintaining a record of marriages, births and deaths. A significant proportion of Punjabi traders in Ballimaran belong to the AH. There are instances of people becoming AH later in life; there are also instances of divisions in the family between AH and non-AH members. Khan contested the elections for the post of the President of the Anjuman twice, losing both times, once in a tie.

Punjabi Phatak, a former palace (*haveli*), and the area where I did much of my fieldwork, is made up of domestic establishments and clustered commercial complexes—shops, restaurants and guesthouses. Most of the rooms that made up this palace have been sold to different owners, and the larger rooms often house more than one shop. The average size of a shop in Punjabi Phatak is 50–80 square feet. These complexes can be seen in most of the *katras* and *kuchas* in Chandni Chowk. A few of the larger *havelis* have become *katras* or *kuchas,* such as Punjabi Phatak.[5] Punjabi Phatak itself is

---

[5] *Haveli* was a palace or a large mansion in the vicinity of the Red Fort for the princes, nobles and the affluent members of the Mughal court. The haveli had gardens, watercourses, courtyards, many rooms and chambers with separate sections for men and women. A *katra* was a locality in which people belonging to the same profession or trade lived. The houses in such a locality were situated within a boundary. A *kucha* was a locality that was related to and named after a prominent person. A kucha had many streets and usually two routes of entry and exit. A *mohalla* is a small neighborhood that has many houses in various streets and lanes. Usually, a main street runs through the mohalla breaking down into many smaller streets, lanes and by-lanes. The lanes and by-lanes usually end in cul-de-sacs. The main street that runs through the mohalla usually leads to the other mohalla and, therefore, is not closed like a katra.

made up of 22 houses and 32 domestic establishments. Every house has more than two shops on the ground floor.[6]

I met Ahmad Khan in June 2006 when I had begun to walk through the various alleys of Punjabi Phatak. He stays on the first floor of a three-storey building along with his wife Ruksana Ahmad, a divorced daughter, called Shabnam, and son, Firoze. Khan's elder sister, an old widowed woman, and her daughter Kulsum and son Nadeem occupy the second floor. The third floor houses Khan's classificatory relatives from his father's side. He is estranged from them. Part of this estrangement is due to property disputes over the ownership of two shops situated on the ground floor of Khan's house. Khan claims that he had given these shops to his father's brother's sons in the mid-1970s after their shops, situated in the Jama Masjid area, had been demolished during the Emergency (1975–77).[7] After his retirement in 1992, Khan asked for these shops to be given back to him. On being refused, he took his case to the Mufti of the Fatehpuri mosque, who ruled in his favour but was unable to enforce his ruling (he calls this case *haqq-talfi*—violation of right—while the respondents call this *haqq bazarya-i-qabzah,* or the right acquired by continuity of possession). Khan then met the Punjabi Anjuman of Ballimaran, who, according to him, promised

---

[6] Ballimaran itself is made up of four distinct segments: Lal Kuan Gali Chabuk Sawar, Haveli Hisamuddin Haider Chhoti Khirki, also known as Gali Qasim Jan, Punjabi Phatak and Gali Jamun Wali. The entire complex is made up of about 70 houses and more than 100 domestic establishments and 150 small shops.

[7] Muslim merchants were particularly affected during the Emergency. In November 1975 bulldozers cleared the entire area around Jama Masjid after a forced eviction ordered by the Delhi Development Authority under its vice-chairman, Jagmohan. He was alleged by the *Indian Express* to have said that he would not allow another Pakistan in Delhi. Jagmohan took the *Indian Express* correspondent, Jawed Laiq to court. Since 1995, the bazaar at Jama Masjid has become a battleground between the Imam of the Masjid, the Waqf Board and various civic authorities.

to have his premises restored to him within six months. But the relationship between him and the Anjuman turned hostile when it became public knowledge that he was a communist. In September 1993, Khan had a recurring dream, in which he saw the Prophet, who showed him the decay of the Ka'aba in Mecca. This was also the time when he began to read Shibli Numani's *Umar al-Faruq*. He promised himself that he would establish a mosque and a small learning centre. His formal conversion to the AH occurred in 1994, when he was admitted into the AH mosque in Ballimaran in the presence of the imam. In 1996 Khan again approached the Anjuman to intercede in a divorce case involving his youngest daughter. Here the Anjuman upheld his plea that his daughter be exempt from *idda* (a period of waiting for four months and ten days before the divorce is finalized) before her divorce became binding.

CONVERSION

The literature on conversion is extensive but this is not the place to provide a review.[8] I will, however, indicate some of its current directions to establish filiations and disjunctions. In the first place, conversion is visualized as a kind of passage—a turning from and to (Austin-Broos 2003: 1). Here, the language of converts expresses new forms of relatedness and the public aspect of this newly inscribed self is defined through the gaze of others. For the convert, conversion negotiates an intimate place in the world (ibid.: 2). Conversion, in this sense, is not a quest for utopia but for habitus. A second direction of analysis sees conversion as shaped by historical experiences and the meaning systems of Islam (Robinson 2003: 6). Religious conversion emerges from religious elites and specialists,

---

[8] For informative accounts see Bruce Lawrence (1985: 106–23); Peter Hardy (1979: 68–99); Zawwar Hussain Zaidi (1989: 93–117); Eaton (1999); Rambo (1999: 259–71).

marking a 'hyper-distinctiveness' around ideas of exclusivity (ibid.).⁹ Exclusivity itself varies—from initiation rituals and dogmas to an immersion in local social practices. In this sense, conversion is theoretically profuse, invoking the novel and playing with difference (ibid.:12–13).

Important as these arguments are, they assume that conversion is from one religion to another, or, at best, absorption of preliterate people into a religious ideology (Eaton 1999:11).[10] The wilful and reflexive transition from a secular world to a religious one has not received attention. This move—from a structure of belief conditioned by secular ideologies, to one coloured by the religious—is neither abrupt nor unmediated. While it is true that conversion assesses the material and imaginary conditions of the convert's future, the focus on the novel also involves the past and its interactions. In effect, the conversion experience highlights a time that is multiple and assembling. Following from this, conversion establishes a multifaceted relationship between itself and discrete social arenas. But there is a tension built into this relationship—between the transcendental promise of conversion and the prosaic texture of everyday situations.

---

[9] Without denying the power of exclusion, it is possible to argue that the symbols of conversion form the basis of universally revered and accepted norms, with the aim of adding to the bonds of political loyalty or submission engendered by armed might and/or economic advantage. Exclusivity, in this sense, is leavened by membership to the *ummah*, hence inclusion, a point overlooked by Robinson.

[10] Eaton says that this process of absorption is divided into two—accretion and reform, but that individual cases of Muslim conversion movements show more complex patterns (1999). In his overview, Rambo (1999: 259–71) presents a kind of cartography of options that explain conversion but what we miss is the attention to the ordinary. The insurrections of people like Ahmad are individual, small-scale and perhaps intensely private acts. But in transforming these private acts into an active mode of public life Ahmad provides us with a way of understanding how contemporary religiosity intersects with and is entangled in the everyday.

In this essay, I trace the way in which a dynamic and heterogeneous temporality is built into the conversion experience of Ahmad Khan, one that entwines the past, present and future. Following from this I suggest that the embodiment of this temporality leads to a kind of split self, through which Ahmad is able to express and practise a radically secular existence together with a religious one. In this splitting Ahmad seems to be located on the margins of the Punjabi traders. Here, I find instructive Lévi-Strauss' (1987: 16–19) discussion of the 'abnormal' as embodying marginality and the split self. Sanity, for Lévi-Strauss, is the ability to balance the division between self and other and those unable to do so live either in the other or within themselves. Individuals who cannot manage this split have access to a 'pure' language, with little reference to the world. The importance of such people is that they complete the global system of signification. That is to say, those on the margins, those with pure language, provide the crucial function of translation between, what Lévi-Strauss calls, different symbolic systems that make up any culture. Such marginals, with 'apparently abnormal modes of behaviour,... figuratively represent certain forms of compromise not available on the collective plane' (ibid., 18). Because they are placed between incompatible symbolic systems they are unable to fully participate in normal social life, but by the same token they are able to articulate the differences. I follow this line of thinking with the following variations. Rather than argue that the convert bridges the gap between different registers of social life, I aim to show that there is an ambiguity and illicit knowledge built into the heart of conversion. This ambiguity conveys the inadequacy of naming fully a change of status, as much as it shows how an environment of suspicion is indicated by conversion. In what follows I trace the conversion experience of Khan into the AH version of Islam. I do this by reading Khan's story of conversion by focusing on the way in which the term 'Muslim' is a floating signifier and a kind of 'quanta of signification' below which there can only be a pointing function.

As floating signifier, the term Muslim accommodates both textual and circumstantial factors and tells a story through other stories, themselves located in bundles of texts and contexts. The protean quality of this name is tied to a self-serving religious language but is, at the same time, riddled with tension between the political and the religious, the global and the local, between those who are of the AH and other Muslims, between Muslims and non-Muslims. Sometimes the term brings together different temporalities; at other times it mediates intimate relations to establish distance. In this way, multiple struggles fall within the ambit of the symbolic imagery of the name. To this extent, the name gathers meaning through a variety of social institutions that engage it, meanings that resonate specifically in the interpretive communities that both generate conversion and receive it.

By building substantially upon his everyday practices of religiosity and drawing on conflicts within his domestic interactions, specifically those that relate to property disputes, Khan proposes the Islam of *Sahih* as a way of communal well being. He argues that *khudi* (self/selfhood) must be imagined as a universalized symbol that invites all Muslims into the *ummah*. What, then, is the utility of the symbolism of conversion? Put in another way, is it necessary to provide a religiously informed reading of the world, as Khan does, at the expense of other analyses that consider class, education, gender, politics and so on? Khan never used the term *tawbah* (repentance, 'metanoia' and thus conversion[11]) to talk of his experience. The term *da'wat* (summons, invitation), referring now to mean active missionary style proselytizing, was used by him to refer to the programmes of education of the AH. This call to adopt

---

[11] See DeWeese: 22.

the Islam of the AH was not part of his discursive elaboration of his experience. *Da'wat* acted as a narrative device to point to contests with those of a different understanding of Islam. His conversion was framed not within the paradigm of Islamizing territory, as it was within that of being a good Muslim. In this latter sense he presented his conversion experience as a change of name. He constantly mentioned that conversion was not a change of 'heart', but an appreciation of the *Sahih*.

In focusing on the name one may argue that we are participating in the purely nominal and superficial character of Islam, and that most Muslims in India, if not the subcontinent, adopted Islam only formally, taking on some external signs and ritual forms (one of the unfortunate by-products of the syncretist argument). The argument is misdirected from three perspectives. First, to underestimate the importance of adopting the self-designation, 'Muslim', is to misunderstand the significance of the spoken word among various Muslim societies in India. The name and its utterances have a sacred character—the correspondence of a thing's name and its reality is often assumed to be a physical and magical link between the name and the named. Here, to call oneself 'Muslim' evokes a sacred history and to adopt a name is to change one's reality. In this sense, there is hardly a deeper conversion than a nominal one.[12]

Second, from the point of view of conversion, the name and its ritual form are linked with sacred power—the power of the

---

[12] I do not wish to suggest that the name 'Muslim' is merely concerned with classification. In his discussion of the relation between personal names and classification, Lévi-Strauss (1966: 181) thinks of the former as transformative codes—'one never names: one classes someone else' (ibid.). While the term 'Muslim' might reflect a classificatory system as well as signify a social person, it also carries a performative and didactic weight. In this sense it constitutes social relations. For a fuller discussion see the volume edited by vom Bruck and Bodenhorn (2006).

external to affect the internal. Sacralized social interaction is the channel for divine grace, where the adoption of Islamic names amounts to an *opening*. Finally, while the adoption of the name endorses Islam as an ideal, it also re-aligns one's orientation to the everyday. I must reiterate that what is important here is not a pure Islam, but that the adoption of Islam, however nominal or superficial, makes the convert also 'native'. From the AH point of view, there is nothing inherently base in converting to Islam for economic or political benefit. The promise of participating in the material benefits enjoyed by the AH is in no way a disreputable inducement to the change of status implied by naming.

COMMUNISM, DREAMS AND THE SPLIT SELF

Khan is in his late-60s, or early 70s. He was born in Delhi and was in his pre-teens at the time of Partition. Before Partition he was enrolled in the Harcourt Butler School. 1947 marked a break of about a year in his schooling and when he went back to his education he shifted to the Crescent Public School. Khan is a tall, balding man, extremely soft-spoken, who has taken to wearing the traditional Muslim dress of kurta-pyjama and prayer cap. He did not always dress this way. By his own account he came to this dress after his conversion dream and found it suited his new status. Khan is an educated man, having completed his masters in Urdu from the Aligarh Muslim University. He married Ruksana Ahmad in 1968, the year he graduated. He refused to deposit money for bride-wealth (*mahr*) or accept the trousseau that accompanied his wife. After his conversion, however, he deposited a sum of Rs 50,000 as *mahr* and had his wife's personal possessions documented. Since 2004, Ruksana Ahmad has been conducting regular Arabic classes for women. The aim is to impart the learning of Quranic Arabic to enable women to read and understand the Quran directly without the assistance of translation or of the clergy. The classes are suspended during Ramzan and resume after Eid. In 2005 Ruksana was diagnosed with a life-threatening disease.

After graduation, Khan was initially an office bearer of the Central Industrial Trade Union (CITU). Two years later he found employment in the Indian Labour Organization, situated in Bombay. As part of his work he was required to keep abreast of the formal rules between employer and employee, act as negotiating agent between union demands and management responses, and in rare instances provide his opinions on the feasibility of 'shut downs'.

Khan was introduced to the work of Karl Marx (he specifically mentions the *Manifesto*) during his student days at AMU. In the second year at the university he became a member of the CPI, and later the CPM and took active part in student union activities. Towards the end of his university career he was sworn to secrecy regarding the life of his friends and colleagues, some of whom were drawn to the Naxalite movement in Bengal. I asked him whether he had thought of joining the Naxalites.[13]

For our type of people that was a dream, but when I became ready to go, an offering in the way of a job presented itself. The party had found work for me in Bombay and I started on my journey. Initially I was part of the Matunga area of the Central Industrial Trade Union (CITU). In 1970 I was employed in the industrial tribunal of the Central Labour Institute (CLI) and became a Director. After that sometimes Byculla, sometimes Mazgoan, sometimes Parel. In Bombay I stayed approximately 20 years, first in Sewri and then in Mazgoan, but I saw Colaba three times (*Hum jaise logon ke liye yeh ek khwab tha. Jab hum tayyar hue, humare liye ek nazrana pesh hua. Party*

---

[13] The following conversations took place during the Ramzan of 2006. The particular interaction that I focus on here occurred in Khan's house and part of it during our walk towards the Fatehpuri mosque. The discussion began late in the afternoon and continued well after the last prayer. The conversation was resumed after the last call of the next day.

ne Bambai men naukari dhoondhi aur hum ravana ho gaye. Pehle CITU ke office men Matunga ki organization ko sambhala. 1970 men CLI ke industrial tribunal men shamil hue. Uske bad kabhi Mazgoan, kabhi Parel, kabhi Byculla. Bambai men takreeban bees sal rahe, par Colaba teen bar dekhe).

Q: What was the nature of your work?
A: Many things, but mainly I had to document cases of complaints brought by workers against management.
Q: What kinds of complaints?
A: Numerous cases. You may say that 90 per cent were concerned with non-payment of overtime to workers. Some dealt with housing problems, others with pension and PF (provident fund).
Q: What kinds of workers were these…textile, leather, dockhands?
A: Mill hands, in Parel and Byculla, but for a year among the Mathadis (dockyard workers in Mazgaon), I think 79–80.

We were interrupted by Firoze returning home after work. Khan excused himself and went to talk to his son in another part of the house. On returning, he explained that he wanted to know whether Firoze had offered the *zuhr namaz* (noon prayer). 'What would happen if he…' I attempted to ask. Anticipating me, Khan said, 'Well he would have to do it now, wouldn't he?' We resumed our earlier conversation after I had supplied the thread.

Q: Were these workers part of a union?
A: They were earlier part of the INTUC (Indian National Trade Union Congress) and some were of the BMS (Bharat Mazdoor Sangh). But they all became members of the Maharashtra Girni Kamgar Union, also known as the Red Flag Union, with Doctor's Saheb's strike.[14] Those days, the union was the

---

[14] Khan is referring to the Bombay textile workers' strike led by Dr Datta

millat (nation), and management, *dawlat* (state), and RMMS (Rashtriya Mill Mazdoor Sangh, or National Mill Workers' Union), the *dalal* (mediator, also meaning, pimp). I also became a member of the MGKU and whenever we went to Parel or Sewri it was as if our lives were in our hands (*sir se kafan bandhe hue the*; literally our heads were covered with a pall).

Q: When did you decide to leave the union?

A: After 1984 the government broke our back and the MGKU became a society of bickering snakes, marked by the flickering of their tongues (*sanpon ki jama'at men zabano ka lapalap*). I was charged with deviation (*inhiraf*). Perhaps they had secret intelligence (*khufiyah khabar*) about my activities.

Q: What activities?

A: See, in '84 we had Bhiwandi and later Delhi. There was an environment of generalized killing (*qatl-e-am*) of workers and religious minorities. When I said that this must be included in the educational programmes of the CLI some thought that I was communal, that I was favouring Muslim workers against Marathi workers...I was transferred to Delhi. In '86 I resigned from the CLI. And then 1992 occurred. After that, you can see the result (*natija*)...A train line runs from 1992 to 2002. It starts in Ayodhya and comes to rest in Godhra. Where it goes next I can't say, but go it will.

Khan refused to elaborate on the 'khufiyah khabar' that had led to his transfer from Bombay to Delhi. During the course of this interaction Khan's wife Ruksana Ahmad interrupted Khan once, asking him to find her medicine. Khan excused himself and went

---

Samant, President of the Maharashtra Girni Kamgar Union. The strike, involving about 250,000 workers, began in January 1982 and lasted 12 to 18 months. An extensive literature, found especially in the *Economic and Political Weekly*, documents the strike.

into another room while Ruksana came and sat next to me. 'He wore his *tawiz* because of me', she said. 'He doesn't have faith in this, but Mufti *sab's* tongue and word give me relief. On his word he wore it (*Unka yakeen nahin hai par Mufti sab ke zaban aur kalam se mujhe sukun milta hai. Unke kahane pe pahan liya*). He gets me L-Dopa from the hospital. It gives me stomach ache.' I asked her what the *tawiz* contained. She said that the Mufti had written a hadith from the Book of Medicine. This hadith would have to be recited by Khan whenever she was taking the honey prescribed and blessed by the Mufti. Khan was a frequent visitor to the Fatehpuri mosque, periodically getting the Mufti to write out a prescription for his wife. Ruksana would drink the honey and also eat the piece of paper on which the Mufti had written his prescription. Khan returned, saying that he could not find the honey, and then muttered that he would have to make another visit to 'that *muchhandar* (idiot)', the Mufti. The time had come for the last prayer and since Ruksana was not feeling well, Khan decided to offer prayers with her in the house, rather than in the mosque. For the prayer a quorum of four people was required, with at least one of the worshippers being from another domestic establishment. In the present instance, Khan's sister's daughter, Kulsum and son Nadeem joined them.

On our way to the mosque I asked Khan why he had to wear the *tawiz* and not his wife. He kept quiet for a while and then said, 'Mufti Muqarram is wise, especially when he sits in his hospital. His interpretation/translation of medicine is acute. He says that the partner's affect on the ailing is necessary. When my wife takes medicine I translate/interpret it into words for her ears (*Mufti Muqarram khirad mand hain, khas tor jab apne shafa khana men baithte hain. Tibia men unka tarjumah tez hai. Kehta hai ke sathi ka asr mariz ke liye hajat mand hai. Jab walida dawai lete hain hum uska tarjumah lafs men karte hain, unke kan ke liye*)'. Laughing, he added, 'but this is only for her benefit. I'm still a materialist, (*dahri*), a "socialist Muslim".

Muqarram is a market inspector and we are supposed to be the protected (*Muqarram muhatsib hai aur hum mahfuz*)'. We had by this time entered a general provisions shop, where Khan bought a bottle of honey and then continued our walk to the Fatehpuri mosque. On entering it, Khan produced an old appointment letter written by the Mufti and we were able to bypass a long queue of people waiting to see him. Khan introduced me to Mufti Muqarram, saying that I was his record keeper (*khatib*). The Mufti laughed and said 'his tongue is acidic but his heart is pure (*inki zaban pe tehzab hai, par inka kaleja pak hai*). Khan handed him the bottle of honey, the Mufti took it to another room and returned with another bottle and a new prescription. 'Tell him about your dream', he told Khan. On our way back, Khan appeared tired and asked me to meet him the next day. 'Come', he said, 'let's have some gulab jamuns. Tomorrow don't eat anything during the day and perhaps we can break our fast together.' After we had eaten the sweet, Khan patted me on the back and said, 'now, how did you find the rounded sweet of the ass (*ab kaise lage gulabi pede gand ke*)'. Before I could say anything, Khan had bid me goodbye.

I met Khan the next evening, having reached his house just after the last call. Ruksana offered me a traditional dish of dates and sweetened milk which are consumed to break the fast. Khan had gone to the AH mosque to offer prayers and was on his way back. After he appeared, he seemed hesitant to talk about his dream but on the urging of Ruksana and Firoze he began his account. Referring to his facetious comment of the last evening, I said I did not look forward to gulab jamuns today, even though I had kept the fast.[15] The retort was swift, 'wise man, your hair has turned

---

[15] Ruksana and Firoze broke into laughter hearing the term gulab jamuns, and Firoze mentioned that it was only his father who could eat the sweets in the house; the others found the association established by his comments disgusting.

gray, but you haven't left being shameless (*miyan, bal pak gayen hain, par badtemizi nahin chore*)'. I was not allowed to take notes or record what he was saying, and the following account is my reconstruction after I had left his house. After Ahmad had finished reciting his dream I asked whether it was consistent with the *Sahih*. I was interested in the issue of coherence that Messick argues for in the 'calligraphic state', where textual domination is organized around a central body of religious texts, memorized and recited by participants. Ruksana and Firoze, both witnesses to his recitation, said that the *ruy'a* is a divine gift and had nothing to do with the *Sahih*. Ahmad argued that the *ruy'a* was an exemplary narrative, but neither autobiographical, nor psychological. It was instead a narrative that demanded acknowledgement from him.

I will present six fragmentary accounts by which I hope to address the name. Two are lead ups to the dream, while the next two present snippets of the dream. The final two fragments present a relation between the word and the body, following his conversion.

Statement 1: In the 1990s, at the end of my career I began to think about where this materialist (*dahri*) philosophy was taking me. One phrase, I don't know who said it, kept ringing in my head— Instead of being the Khans to the west let us be Muslim slaves.

Statement 2: I began to think of the meaning of the term 'Muslim', but it was not in my natural disposition (*fitrat*) to recognize any formulas of blessing (*durud*). I asked a dear friend of mine, Manas, whether he had thought of religion (*dharma*). I think he understood. Both of us had been fellow travellers in the working class movement.

Statement 3: The dreams started with the anti-Babri movement, flashes of the Ka'aba and sometimes of Buraq (the mount that carried the Prophet to his heavenly journey, depicted with a female head and a peacock's tail).

Statement 4: Then in September '93, I saw Hazrat Peghambar,

who showed me the decay of the Ka'aba and asked me to build a mosque here.

Statement 5: I had already begun to read Numani's *Umar al-Faruq*. Hazrat Umar mentions five *suras* above others—Baqara, Nisa, Ma'ida, Hajj and Nur as ways of overcoming all differences among various Muslim groups. When you recite these *suras* you change colour—they are ways of training one's breath (*habs-i-dam*).

Statement 6: If you recite the *Shahada* long enough, there comes a time when the Shahada recites you. I also spent nights in supererogatory prayers (*nafl*). In Ramzan, during *saum* (fasting from daybreak to sunset) I find a place for meditation (*khalwat*, secluded place) where I can remember/recite (*zikr*) prayers from the longer *suras* (such as Yusuf and Yunus). Shahada and zikr, Shahada and zikr—if you practise this you are Muslim.

Working with fundamentalist Christian missionaries and their converts, Schieffelin (2002) shows that the process of conversion introduces new speech genres, grammatical and lexical innovations and new forms of verbal interaction. Such changes punctuate a sense of time (ignorant past/enlightened present) and an awareness of a millennial future. The experience of conversion saturates everyday talk and the convert is marked by new temporal sensibilities. This Christian scheme of conversion draws on a semiotic that seems to be an imposition by others on the convert and is marked by a series of deliverance rituals that break with the past.[16] Khan's account, too, marks time, but we find a braiding of the past in the present. Unlike missionary-style proselytizing, he presents his story, not as an imposition but a translation of an inner state. I will briefly discuss this translation.

---

[16] See Webb Keane (2007) for a discussion on conversion histories in Indonesia. These rituals insist upon the 'heart' as more important than the law, emphasizing content over form and insisting that religion is a matter of personal belief.

Apart from the ostensive political content of the first two statements (Muslims against the west, communism against religion), what I find interesting is the linking of the term Muslim to *fitrat* (natural disposition) and *durud* (blessings, usually from the Prophet). The term Muslim is further elaborated through the dream statements (3 and 4), where we find an association between the dream, the Ka'aba and Buraq, ending finally with seeing Prophet Muhammad. The next two series of statements elaborate what it means to be Muslim, by mentioning five Quaranic verses and their impress on the body. The final statement establishes the importance of praying and remembering and points, I think, to an ethic of the self . We might, then be able to constitute a preliminary series that would look something like this:

Muslim—fitrat—durud—Ka'aba—Buraq—Prophet—suras—habs-i-dam—shahada—nafl—saum—zikr

This series is not a simple movement from one term to another. Rather, the process of knitting them together shows how a 'pure language' comes to stand for conversion. Its moral imperative is that it incorporates the dreamer by allowing a mode of reference that is internal to the metonymic chain. In this sense, the term 'Muslim' achieves fruition. Emerging from the metonymic chain, the term has a significance that extends into the everyday social world of Khan.[17] In the language of Lévi-Strauss, it is marked by a 'signifier surfeit', linking social domains and insuring cultural coherence; the term integrates because it unifies a voice that is dispersed across social contexts and is therefore an element of social equilibrium. Persuasive as this argument is, we must recognize that Khan's dream statements are also performative: they require the sincere intention of the speaker/dreamer. In his dream sequence, the 'I' is

---

[17] For a relation of dreams to events, see Iain Edgar (2006: 263–72).

the subject, but this subject is filled out only when the dream is received by others. The first and immediate function of the dream is that it modifies Khan's situation. In acknowledging it, Khan gives himself a new obligation. This obligation is not the consequence of his words since he cannot attribute meaning to them prior to the dream sequence. In this sequence, the term Muslim is a conventional signifier but its usage depends upon the agreement of others. I have developed this argument elsewhere.[18]

From a second point of view, the term Muslim for Khan depends upon a knowledge lodged within him, a knowledge over which he has scarce critical faculties but one he must acknowledge. That is to say, Khan does not have an integral voice. While through the dream sequence he assumes the name Muslim, through his communist past, the term is also charged with suspicion. The self here is split, a self that responds to everyday conventions and also one that rests on becoming foreign to itself. Let me point to the ways in which we can understand this foreignness. In the first instance, the term Muslim is placed within an understanding of deviation and secret knowledge (*inhiraf*). Here, the term is explicitly political, set within the backdrop of the textile strike, the disturbances of 1984, culminating in the destruction of the mosque. In *African Islam*, Rene Bravmann (1983), discussing the masks in Poro dance performance, argues that they both conceal and reveal. The concealed part of the masks serves to protect others from the performance, especially from the sacred words that are part of the performance. Deviation

---

[18] Briefly, this argument develops a form of intimacy through which Khan comes to relate to other Muslims of Punjabi Phatak. Here, the dream is a visual depiction for that which has no visual means. It is, in the words of Al-Bagdadi (2006: 138), a 'vision without visual representation'. Furthermore, dreams are not only a visual experience for the dreamer, for they conjure up a visual presence for listeners. Such presence shows itself in oral form, which then becomes available for correct interpretation.

and secret knowledge suggest a similar process in the case of Khan. To espouse the cause of Muslims in a communist organization invites a cryptic encoding that is both foreign and illegible to him. But illegibility also points to provisional transformations in his elaboration of the term Muslim.

This transformation is found in the context of his wife's illness, especially around the *tawiz* and his opinion of the Mufti. The *tawiz*, on the surface in contact with Khan's body, but invisible to others, carries inscribed magic squares with Arabic letters and numbers, with specific references to the Book of Medicine, and to the practice that must be deployed to make it (the *tawiz*) effective in performance. The body animates this practice from the inside, but is also possessed by activating powers transmitted to it by words and substances concealed by the *tawiz*. Furthermore, the literal ingestion of the word by Ruksana complements this activation. In this sense, we find an 'underneath' of the material object. There is, yet, a deeper understanding of what lies beneath the surface. The dream points to the primacy of the concealed in understanding the visible. Classic anthropological accounts (I have in mind E.B. Tylor's *Religion in Primitive Culture*, 1970 [1871]) use words such as animism, fetishism, magic, to refer to these forces through which the material is seen as the vehicle for the spiritual, a separation that Asad reminds us is part of a European and Christian genealogy of the anthropology of religion. In this way we can understand the mutual constitution and suspicion that lies in the interface between the visible and hidden forces of conversion in the life of Ahmad Khan.

References

Alam, Muzaffar. *The Languages of Political Islam: India 1200–1800*. Chicago: University of Chicago Press.

Al-Bagdadi, Nadia. 2006. The Other Eye: Sight and Insight in Arabic Classical Dream Literature. *The Medieval History Journal*. 9: 116–42.

Annual Report of the National Minority Commission, Delhi: National Minorities Commission. 1999.

Asad, Talal. 1986. *The Idea of an Anthropology of Islam*. Washington DC: Centre for Contemporary Arab Studies.

Austin-Broos, Diane. 2003. 'The Anthropology of Conversion: An Introduction' in Andrew Buckser and Stephan J. Glazer, eds., *The Anthropology of Religious Conversion*. Maryland: Rowman and Littlefield Publishers, pp. 1–14.

Bravmann, Rene. 1984. *African Islam*. Washington DC: Smithsonian Books.

Constituent Assembly of India, Legislative Debates, November-December 1949. Delhi: Manager of Publications, 1949.

DeWeese, Devin. 1994. *Islamization and Native Religion in the Golden Horde*. Pennsylvania: Pennsylvania State University Press.

Duderija, Adis. 2007. 'Neo-Traditional Salafis Qur'an-Sunnah Hermeneutic and the Construction of a Normative Muslimah Image', *Hawwa*, Vol. 5, No. 23: 289–323.

Eaton, Richard. 1993. 'Approaches to the Study of Conversion in Islam in India', in Richard M. Martin (ed.): *Approaches to Islam in Religious Societies*. Tucson: University of Arizona Press, pp. 106–23.

Edgar, Iain R. 2006. 'The True Dream in Contemporary Islamic/Jihadist Dreamwork: A Case Study of the Dreams of Taliban Leader Mullah Omar', *Contemporary South Asia*, Vol. 15, No. 3, 2006: 263–72.

Hardy, Peter. 1979. 'Modern European and Muslim Explanations of Conversion to Islam in South Asia: A Preliminary Survey of the Literature', in Nehemia Lévitzion, ed., *Conversion to Islam*, New York: Holmes and Meier Publishers, 1979, pp. 68–99.

http://al-sunnah.com

Jackson, Sherman A. 'On the Boundaries of Theological Tolerance in Islam: Abu Hamid al-Ghazali's Faysal al Tafriqa'. Oxford: Oxford University Press.

Keane, Webb. 2007. *Christian Moderns: Freedom and Fetish in the Mission Encounter*. Berkeley: University of California Press.

Lévi-Strauss, Claude. 1966. *The Savage Mind*. London: Weidenfield and Nicolson.

Lévi-Strauss, Claude. 1987. *Introduction to the Work of Marcel Mauss*. Trans. Felicity Baker. London: Routledge and Kegan Paul.

Messick, Brinkley. 1996. *The Calligraphic State: Textual Domination and History in a Muslim Society*. Berkeley: University of California Press.

Metcalf, Barbara. 1982. *Islamic Revival in British India*. Princeton: Princeton University Press.

——— 2004. *Islamic Contestations: Essays on Muslims in India and Pakistan*. Delhi: Oxford University Press.

Rambo, Lewis R. 1999. 'Theories of Conversion: Understanding and Interpreting Religious Change', *Social Compass*, Vol. 46, No. 3, 259–71.

Robinson, Rowena and Sathianathan Clarke, eds., 2003. *Religious Conversion in India: Moods, Motivations and Meanings*. Delhi: Oxford University Press.

Roy, Olivier. 2005. *Globalised Islam: The Search for a New Ummah*. Delhi: Rupa and Company.

Sanyal, Usha. 1999. *Devotional Islam and Politics in British India: Ahmad Riza Khan Barelwi and His Movement, 1870–1920*. Delhi: Oxford University Press.

Schieffelin, Bambi B. 2002. 'Marking Time: The Dichotomizing Discourse of Multiple Temporalities', *Current Anthropology* 43: S5–S16.

Tylor, Edward Burnett. 1958 [1871]. *Religion in Primitive Culture*. New York: Harper and Row.

vom Bruck, Gabriele and Barbara Bodenhorn, eds. 2006. *The Anthropology of Names and Naming*. Cambridge: Cambridge University Press.

Wiktorowicz, Quintan. 2005. 'The Salafi Movement: Violence and the Fragmentation of Community', in Miriam Cooke and Bruce B. Lawrence, eds., *Muslim Networks: From Medieval Scholars to Modern Feminists*. New Delhi: Permanent Black, pp. 208–34.

Zaidi, Zawwar Hussain. 'Conversion to Islam in South Asia: Problems and Analysis', *American Journal of Islamic Social Science*, Vol. 6, No. 1, 1989, pp. 93–117.

Zaman, Muhammad Qasim. 2004. *The Ulama in Contemporary Islam: Custodians of Change*. Delhi: Oxford University Press.

Lévi-Strauss and Evolutionary Theory

MAURICE BLOCH

The text which follows is that of lecture given in India as part of a celebration of Lévi-Strauss' hundredth birthday. It was addressed to a general academic audience many of whom were anthropologists or sociologists but there were others from different backgrounds. Even among the social scientists, many came from very different scholarly traditions and I wanted to combat certain hostile misconceptions that I believe are common in the English speaking university world including India. I took the opportunity to step back and to think about Lévi-Strauss' work as though I had just come to it for the first time and to think about his contribution in the most fundamental and general way possible.

The first thing to say about Lévi-Strauss is that he is an anthropologist. This was the term that he chose on his return to France after the war. He might have chosen other words such as sociologist or ethnologist, which would have linked him to older and more established French traditions for a social anthropologist, but he chose anthropology. Such words do not indicate subject matters, rather they point to academic traditions. Thus, it is not surprising that, for example, they mean somewhat different things in American English, British English and Indian English. In France Lévi-Strauss' choice meant that he wanted to place his work within the framework defined by the early English-speaking founders of the subject and this is how I see his work.

As an academic subject, anthropology developed in the later part of the nineteenth century with the extraordinary ambition of being *the* science of mankind, a science that was therefore going to define what human nature was, as opposed, for example, to the nature of other animals. In order to do this, this science would use whatever evidence was available from archaeology, palaeontology, human biology, linguistics and data about cultural and social variation among contemporaries in order to answer fundamental questions concerning human kind.

Lévi-Strauss' choice of being an anthropologist, in what we might call the 'strong' sense of the word, in the middle of the twentieth century was an anomaly, especially for someone working in the field which has been roughly covered by social and cultural anthropology. This is so all the more because anthropology meant, for the early anthropologist, studying human evolution.

We have learnt much more than is usually acknowledged from the early anthropologists, the founders of the subject in the late nineteenth-century; those writers whom, I believe, Lévi-Strauss resembles, but they also got an awful lot wrong. Thus, the main thrust of twentieth-century anthropology has been on refuting their theories. Perhaps because of this, perhaps because of other reasons, the subsequent history of anthropology has been, almost entirely negative... one of retreat. Although we have accumulated a great deal of data in all the fields from which the early anthropologists sought evidence, the fundamental theoretical ambition of the subject has never stopped diminishing, so that, finally, in the last part of the twentieth century, we have arrived at a stage when it was possible for a group of scholars to claim, as their greatest theoretical glory, to have no theory at all.

Against this defeatist background the work of Lévi-Strauss stands in sharp contrast. He has always remained an anthropologist in the original sense of the word. But, if he has maintained the definition of the subject as the nineteenth-century founders understood it, he has done this while, at the same time, criticizing in the most fundamental way possible the assumptions that lay behind most familiar evolutionary theories of the past or of the present. As we shall see the basis of his criticism is that the early evolutionary writers had ignored the most evident evolutionary fact about *Homo sapiens,* that is, the implications of the kind of mind evolution has created for our species.

When I consider his contribution with 'a view from afar', to use the title of one of his books, it is clear to me that throughout his work he has been proposing a coherent theory about the evolution of mankind and about human nature that is just as bold as that of any of the founders of the discipline. What I want to do here, then, is to lay bare this general theory. This, however, requires a certain amount of distancing from the texts for a number of reasons. One is because other anthropologists, deep in their retreat mode, have almost wilfully ignored Strauss' most fundamental propositions and refused to discuss them. As a result these have fallen into the background. This may be said even for his own later work. Another reason is due to the character of the man, the result of a characteristic shyness which is best captured by that untranslatable French word 'pudeur'. This has make him hide his boldest claims a little, and this has led him to leave these themes undeveloped as though he was subsequently ashamed to have been so daring.

But, since I am not Strauss, I have no such inhibitions and I shall attempt to expose what lies behind his work in a way that he might well consider vulgar. I believe that, in spite of a change in emphasis, his fundamental orientation has held steady throughout his work.

What do I mean by 'evolutionary' here? If we ignore certain aspects of his earlier work, Lévi-Strauss' work implies the usual rejection of the nineteenth-century idea that different contemporary people around the world somehow represent different stages in the history of mankind. All living human beings are obviously just as distant from the first humans. What interests him is the variety of people around the world. This observation of variety, however, is not simply in order to marvel at cultural and social diversity but to use this as a tool to understand the nature of human beings. Lévi-Strauss wants to understand human beings and that means understanding what their evolutionary history means for the way we are. What I mean by Lévi-Strauss being an evolutionist is therefore the same as what he meant by being an anthropologist. He is seeking a naturalist account, but not one that uses naturalism as an excuse for bypassing human specificity.

I start with an unorthodox interpretation of his first major work, published significantly in 1949, four years after the defeat of Nazi Germany: *The Elementary Structures of Kinship*.

I propose that this book contains a reflection, and a rejection, of a take on human nature which we would now call socio-biology, but which was already explicit at the time of writing and before, in the precursor of socio-biology: eugenics. This theory was derived from the union of Darwinian natural selection with modern genetics and had been applied to humans and kinship. Putting it simply, the synthesis implied that the most successful individuals were those who produced the greatest number of viable offspring. This evolutionary fact was then used by some to explain the anthropological finding that in all human societies the mutual bonds uniting kinsmen are strong. According to the eugenicists, this was because kinship ties were derived from the genetic link between parents and children, which itself was derived from the parents' evolutionary interest in spreading their genes. This, taken together with the then common assumption that early societies were kinship-based, could be taken to mean that the urge to further one's bloodline over others was the natural and inevitable basis of society. A political interpretation of such a reading of eugenics, not the only one by a long way, associated it with the worst forms of racism and Nazism.

I argue that Lévi-Strauss in his book on kinship maintains that such a view reduces human society to 'blood ties' and concentrating on the selfish motivation of maintaining them misses the very essence of what it is to be human. If we use the perhaps unfortunate terminology that he chose, we can say that this eugenics created a view of humans that misses the fact that humans have passed from nature to culture, in other words that our society is quite different from those of other animals, since it is based on conscious contract and not on blood ties. This emphasis on contract as the defining factor in human evolution inevitably leads to a consideration of the characteristics of the human mind and how this can create such a different kind of evolutionary history from that normally envisaged for other animals or that imagined by the nineteenth-century anthropologists. The emphasis on contract leads to the emphasis on the specificity of the human mind and it is this which is the basis of Strauss' evolutionary theory.

To argue such a key role for the rejection of eugenics in the development of Lévi-Strauss' theory of kinship may seem odd in that the words racism or Nazism are, as far as I know, never used. I propose that racist reading of eugenics is the elephant in the room. However, I do not want to argue that the rejection of Nazi ideas is in any way an explanation of Lévi-Strauss' theory, rather it is a tool that enabled him to construct it.

The starting point of the book on kinship is a consideration of rules prohibiting incest and of the universal obligation to reciprocate.

For him these pan-human rules, which take a variety of forms, have the effect that human society cannot be based on blood ties; rather people create, through their intellect, complex systems of exchange between genealogically unrelated people.

The ontological status of incest and reciprocity in his work is ambiguous. In the case of the former, Lévi-Strauss seems to want to deny any instinctive grounding, while, in the case of the latter, he pushes for such a basis. He suggests that the combination of the incest taboo and the reciprocity instinct are merely tools that can then be used in the creation of an infinite variety of social systems. Thus the main body of the book illustrates by means of numerous ethnographic examples how, first, the incest taboo requires out marriage and, second, how, because of the human reciprocity instinct, this need to marry out leads to the definition of groups and roles which become ever more complex and form the basis of social classifications in terms of which society functions. These creations, which are the social systems we know, are thus the product of the activity of human minds using these tools. However, we must remember what, according to this theory, has made such creations possible. This is the kind of evolved brain which makes the shape of our head so different from that of a Chimpanzee. The fact of the peculiarity of our brain does not, however, account for the products of our brain: those complex kinship systems, any more than a Louis the Sixteenth chest of drawers may be explained by the toolbox of the cabinetmaker. He was thus able to argue, at the same time, that human social systems cannot be explained by a natural drive to look after blood relatives, as socio-biologists would have done, and at the same time that we cannot forget the evolutionary biological basis that enables such systems to be created.

I am therefore suggesting that the emphasis on alliance-based kinship systems, which characterizes *The Elementary Structures of Kinship*, something which has so fascinated and puzzled many anthropologists, is not simply a technical anthropological matter, but that it is an aspect of the demonstration of a fundamental theory about human evolution, albeit one which is also a criticism of the type of anthropological evolutionism which had previously been prevalent. What is being said is that because humans have brains that enable them to pass ideas one to another and across the generations, they are caught in systems of their own creations, they are caught in human history which is quite different from the natural history of species that do not have this specialized brain.

Putting the matter like this makes Lévi-Strauss seem very similar to the Boasian anthropological theories to which he had been exposed and which he had, to a certain extent, admired during his stay in the USA during the war. However, the similarity is limited. The American anti-evolutionism of the Boasians was, in most of their cases, total. What such Boasians as Margaret Mead, Ruth Benedict and Alfred Kroeber were arguing for, was that, because humans were cultural beings, we could simply forget about the influence of biology and therefore about evolution. Culture made humans 'super-organic', if we are to use Kroeber's term. This is not Lévi-Strauss' position.

It is important to stress the fundamental difference in the understanding of what is culture in his work and in that of the Boasian cultural anthropologists. For them culture is the system through which we understand the world, it therefore exists before we are capable of any thought or action. It is a kind of cage within which we live and of whose existence we are unaware because we can only be *within* it. By contrast, for Lévi-Strauss, culture is a continually moving *process* being reproduced and also transformed. It is a process that takes place in human minds. If we remember the famous quotation that Geertz borrows from Weber; that Man is an animal suspended in webs of meaning that he himself has spun, we find that the Boasians, and Geertz himself, concentrate on the suspension while Lévi-Strauss concentrates on the spinning. As a result it is inevitable that, unlike the former, he considers we must also pay attention to the mental action such an activity requires. We must consider the workings of the brain.

This is what explains the connection between the earlier book on kinship and what is probably Lévi-Strauss' most famous work, for anthropologists at least, *The Savage Mind*. In the first book he had emphasized how human kinship was different from the kinship systems of other living things, both in form and in kind. This was because of the naturally evolved characteristic of the Homo Sapiens' mind.

In a similar way *The Savage Mind* argues for the relevance of the neurological workings of the evolved human brain for the topics that had and have always concerned social and cultural anthropologists, but he also implies a fundamental criticism of those scientists who see in its working a *direct* explanation of human society and culture.

Lévi-Strauss' argument for the relevance to anthropology of the scientific studies on the working of the mind/brain is straightforward and had already been explained unambiguously in a number of his earlier writings. In order to inform himself about these disciplines Lévi-Strauss had quite naturally turned to a variety of cognitive sciences such as psychology, neurology, artificial intelligence, cognitive linguistics, in much the same way as he had turned towards developmental psychology and primatology in order to understand reciprocity in *The Elementary Structures of Kinship*. Someone like Kroeber would never have done such a thing.

The image Lévi-Strauss obtains from his study of these subjects is of a mind/brain that resembles a Turing machine. Of course, nowadays, given the advances that have been made in our understanding of the working of the brain, his image is old fashioned but it was very sophisticated for its time, especially when compared to the simple stimulus/response psychology of behaviourism that dominated. Interestingly his psychological theory is similar in a number of ways to the theories that Piaget was in the process of developing at the time—Lévi-Straussian 'structure' resembles Piagetian 'equilibration'. This is so even though L-S hardly ever refers to Piaget's work.

What makes the parallel with Piaget particularly interesting, however, is not just the points of similarity but also the fundamental differences. It is not difficult to imagine the twin related criticism he would make of the Piagetian approach. Piaget never seriously takes into account the fact that the child lives already situated within a constructed social world nor the fact that the world in which the child grows up, whether it be the material world, or the people with which the child interacts, is already culturally structured. The Piagetian child has often been characterized as a lone scientist. She appears to observe the world through her perceptive capacities and only then makes sense of it, as though, by herself. If Lévi-Strauss had thought about the growing child, something which as far as I know he never did, he would have emphasized how the material world in which the child develops is the product of the actions of other human beings who have made it according to their historically created aesthetic, practical and ethical conceptions. And, furthermore, he would have added that the people who had made this environment had made it in terms of the concepts of those who surrounded them as children or as adults. The people who surround the child are similarly the product of other people and so on through the flow of history. The relation to the world available to perception is thus always, to a lesser or greater extent, mediated by culture. In other words, the child is always in the midst of the flow of history. It thus becomes rhetorically possible for Lévi-Strauss to assert that there is a sense in which, instead of allowing our theoretical imagination to concentrate on the image of individual people thinking myth, we should also imagine the myth themselves living though and *via* people.

This emphasis on people being always situated within the flows of culture and history is the source of the originality of Lévi-Strauss's psychological theory. In contrast to the Boasians he insists on the need to think of culture as a process in which the individuals are actively involved but he also insists that the individual mental process only occurs within processes that transcend the individual. The analysis of a process within processes is captured by one of his most productive ideas which he indicates by the word 'transformation'.

If the rather mechanical way in which transformations are described in Lévi-Strauss' work in terms of inversions, nesting and so on is misleading, and not in accord with what we now know, the core of the very idea of transformation is most valuable. It is that culture is at every stage a matter of reinvention and recreation not just of transmission. Every individual receives and recreates. If that individual reproduces exactly what he or she has received this is just as much an act of creation as if he or she modified it. Culture is thus a multitude of acts of individual cognitive neurological creation of already existing material that is in an endless process of transformation.

Here I would like to emphasize two interesting implications that flow from his way of seeing things. The first is that the image of 'bounded cultures', a representation that necessarily follows from the view of culture as a 'framework' within which action and thought take place, is unacceptable. The cultural process has no boundary; any interruption in communication between neighbours can only be temporary. Furthermore, it is not simply that cultures flow into each other without any real boundaries; it is that the gradients that can be established for any particular item do not map one on another. If we take the example of myth, which was the subject of the massive four-volume study usually referred to by its French title *Mythologiques,* we find that the different myths known by any individual will each one link up with those known by others, but for each case along quite different patterns. Thus, it is not only that for him there are no boundaries, it is that there is no possible localization of 'cultures' as coherent systems. This is a state of affairs which some sociologists seem to believe has only occurred in the modern world, yet for Lévi-Strauss this lack of orderly division of mankind into bounded groups is as characteristic of the pre-contact Amerindian world as it is of any time anywhere since it has always characterized the history of mankind since the very beginning.

The other implication of the notion of transformation concerns the nature of this cultural material that is being continually reinvented. If we recall, for an instant, the developmental story outlined by Piaget, in it we imagine the child perceiving the world and then deducing from his observations general abstract principles which then form the basis of ever more general theories. This story resembles the traditional view of the scientific method. Lévi-Strauss argues that this is misleading: the child never develops from a pre-cultural state to a cultural state. The child, from the very beginning, is already in a cultural world and thinks with already made concepts and systems about the real world. What we need to study is not, therefore, the evolution of a mind/brain adapted to operate from a zero cognitive starting point but the evolution of a mind/brain adapted to operate *within* the flow of history. This is what Lévi-Strauss is struggling to define in *The Savage Mind,* though I do not think he has gone much further than specifying what needs to be taken into account for such an approach. He has, however, taken a major step in the right direction.

In conclusion let me return to the decision Lévi-Strauss made when he chose the term 'anthropology' in the context of the France of the late 1940s. It meant that he saw what he was doing as part of the general enterprise of a science that was going to understand the nature of human beings in a broad evolutionary framework. In doing this, he was going against the trend of the time, a trend that was moving towards the abandonment of this broad aim. For him, although his work was going to principally take place in that sub-section of anthropology that was called cultural anthropology in the USA and social anthropology in Britain, it was, nonetheless, not going to be bounded, it was going to retain the original ambition of anthropology as an integrated science. He was critical in a fundamental way of all the evolutionary anthropology that had gone before and that was still surviving. He was not concerned with the older evolutionary anthropology that spent its energy in placing different contemporary groups in a pseudo-historical ranking. He was rejecting models of humans that forgot about the revolutionary implications of the human brain. Understanding the implication of the human brain needed to be central to anthropology. However, the available work in psychology of his time was also found wanting because it misrepresented people as outside the cultural-historical process. His stress on the crucial importance of ethnography addresses this. The contribution of ethnography is to force theoreticians to deal with the unique specificity of actual human groups and their thought so that they come up with a theory that does not replace people, as they live their lives within the cultural process, with ciphers outside history, created by the psychological laboratory. He concentrates on Amerindians, not only because he is attracted to their culture, but also because they furnish an example of people with extremely low population densities who live in close interaction with other living species and thus give us an inkling of what the human condition has been for at least 99 per cent of its history.

What we have therefore in the work of Lévi-Strauss is a study of the kind of people evolution has produced and this has to centrally be concerned with the human mind because that is what distinguishes our species. He asks: what have been the implications of this human mind for the natural history of the species? He gives an answer through the common rhetorical device of criticizing the work of others, in this case the early anthropologists, the American cultural anthropologists, and psychologists such as Piaget. These criticisms aim, above all, to stress what these other scholars have missed out in their attempt to characterize human evolution, in their anthropology in other words. In stressing how Lévi-Strauss' work has continued to be part of the general enterprise of anthropology, the term he had chosen for his chair at the college de France, I have wanted to show how different he is from what became the general subsequent historical drift of the subject. In some cases anthropology has even become simply a parochial concern with anthropologists and the professional practice of anthropology rather than a concentration of what the subject was studying.

Lévi-Strauss' work throughout the twentieth century has thus been an oddity because he has remained true to the original calling of anthropology and such a position is an oddity now. Under the label cultural and social anthropology a very wide range of different types of research is being undertaken, much of which is very valuable and serious but, what is often missing, is the general fundamental anthropology that Lévi-Strauss has carried on and forward throughout his long career.

Or rather anthropology has continued but largely outside anthropology departments. It has carried on because the fundamental anthropological questions which the early anthropologists raised still fascinate all normal human beings, with the possible exception of those who are found in social and cultural anthropology departments. In a sense this does not matter. I mentioned before labels such as anthropology, sociology, ethnology, etc., are arbitrary. There is however a problem with this new enthusiasm for anthropology, in the sense Lévi-Strauss has understood it, manifested by biologists, neurologists, philosophers even. It is that those working in such disciplines do not do what he stressed was necessary, they do not continually bruise their theories against the complexity and the variety of the situations which the disciplines of anthropology have been good at bringing to the fore. They are often running the risk of repeating all the old mistakes.

In my view what is needed is the continuing presence in anthropology departments of anthropologists, who are evolutionary anthropologists in the sense Lévi-Strauss has been. This should not be the only thing that goes on, but it should remain the core and continuing to study his work will be one way of ensuring this.

What is needed therefore is the renewal of the fruitful tension that is so central in his work between the complexity which comes from thinking about human beings in the real histories and cultural flows in which they find themselves and the need to think in general terms about the kind of animal human beings are. Those who do this in anthropology departments are rare but it seems to me that very recently they have begun to increase again and because of this I begin to be hopeful that Lévi-Strauss' work is not going to be, what it sometimes resembles, a grand immobile statue in a public park, but more like the plants that grow around the stone monument and, sometimes, in the process of their passing, spread their seeds.

REFERENCES

Lévi-Strauss, Claude. 1992. *View from Afar*, Chicago: Chicago University Press.

———. 1971. *Elementary Structures of Kinship*, Boston: Beacon Press.

———. 1966. *The Savage Mind*, Chicago: Chicago University Press.

———. 1964. 1966. 1968. 1971. *Mythogiques*, Paris: Plon.

Appendix
Claude Lévi-Strauss' Main Works

1948. *La vie familiale et sociale des Indiens Nambikwara.* Paris, Société des Américanistes.

1949. *Les structures élémentaires de la parenté.* Paris, La Haye, Mouton & Co. (*The Elementary Structures of Kinship*, ed., Rodney Needham, trans. J. H. Bell, J. R. von Sturmer, and Rodney Needham, 1969).

1950.'Introduction à l'œuvre de Marcel Mauss', in Marcel Mauss, *Sociologie et anthropologie.* Paris, PUF.

1955. *Tristes tropiques.* Paris, Plon, collection Terre Humaine.

1958. *Anthropologie structurale.* Paris, Plon. (*Structural Anthropology*, trans. Claire Jacobson and Brooke Grundfest Schoepf, 1963).

1961 (1952). *Race et histoire.* Paris, Gonthier.

1962a. *La pensée sauvage.* Paris, Plon. (*The Savage Mind*, 1966).

1962b. *Le totémisme aujourd'hui.* Paris, Presses Universitaires de France. (*Totemism*, trans. Rodney Needham, 1963).

1964. *Mythologiques, I. Le cru et le cuit.* Paris, Plon. (1964, *The Raw and the Cooked*, 1969).

1966. *Mythologiques, II. Du miel aux cendres.* Paris, Plon. (*From Honey to Ashes*, 1973).

1968. *Mythologiques, III. L'origine des manières de table.* Paris, Plon. (1968, *The Origin of Table Manners*, 1978).

1971. *Mythologiques, IV. L'homme nu.* Paris, Plon. (1971, *The Naked Man*, 1981).

1973. *Anthropologie structurale deux.* Paris, Plon. (*Structural Anthropology, Vol. II*, trans. Monique Layton, 1976).

1975. *La voie des masques* (2 vol.). Genève, A. Skira (réédition augmentée, Plon, 1979) (*The Way of the Masks*, trans. Sylvia Modelski, 1982).

1983. *Le regard éloigné*. Paris, Plon. (*A View From Afar*).
1984. *Paroles données*. Paris, Plon. (*Anthropology and Myth: Lectures, 1951–1982*, trans. Roy Willis, 1987).
1985. *La potière jalouse*. Paris, Plon. (*The Jealous Potter*, trans. Bénédicte Chorier, 1988).
1991. *Histoire de Lynx*. Paris, Plon. (*The Story of Lynx*, trans. Catherine Tihanyi, 1996).
1996. *Regarder, écouter, lire*. Paris, Plon. (*Look, Listen, Read*, trans. Brian Singer, 1997).